POLITICS, PROPERTY AND LAW

in the

Philippine

Uplands

Melanie G. Wiber

Wilfrid Laurier University Press

Canadian Cataloguing in Publication Data

Wiber, Melanie, 1954-
  Politics, property and law in the Philippine
uplands

Includes bibliographical references and index.
ISBN 0-88920-222-2

1. Ibaloi (Philippine people). 2. Property
(Ibaloi law). I. Title.

DS666.I12W5 1993   306'.089'9921   C93-093986-7

Copyright © 1993

Wilfrid Laurier University Press
Waterloo, Ontario, Canada
N2L 3C5

Cover design by Connolly Design Inc.

Printed in Canada

Politics, Property and Law in the Philippine Uplands has been produced from a manuscript supplied in electronic form by the author.

Table of Contents

List of Illustrations

Maps

Photographs

(All photographs were taken by the author and her husband and used by courtesy of them.)

List of Tables

Preface

This book documents diachronic processes affecting the property system of a Philippine tribal group from the Cordillera Central in Northern Luzon (see Map 1). It examines several broad lines of inquiry which are interrelated: the organization of a non-Western property system, the effect of political incorporation and economic integration on this system, the consequences of legal pluralism and the individual purposive strategies which make use of such pluralism, and finally, what all of this suggests for anthropological theory and method in the study of property systems.

I lived in the Philippines from September 1983 until August 1984; much of that time was spent living and working in one small, Ibaloi community. I also visited other towns in the province of Benguet (see Map 2) and benefitted from a close association with the Cordillera Studies Center at the University of the Philippines Baguio Campus. The ongoing research of this institution and the people involved in it were particularly helpful in putting the community-specific findings of my research into a broader perspective.

I was originally interested in the relationship between the indigenous organization of irrigation and the rural development potential of irrigation groups. My approach was to find a community with a long history of irrigated rice production and to investigate the social organization which facilitated it. By necessity, this involved examining property rights, particularly access to resources such as land and water. Property-system research became property-law research. I was acquainted with the broad outlines of the Ibaloi property system from my reading; they rely on a combination of productive techniques involving rice terraces, swidden fields, fruit and coffee orchards and gold mines. I was not prepared, however, for the complexity of legal notions of rights and responsibilities which affect individual access to the above resources. The study of this complexity led to an interest in how the property system had developed. As the Ibaloi are a people with a rich sense of tribal history relying in turn on an appreciation of the role of individual historical figures, it is not surprising that the role of individual purposive strategies began to take on significance in my understanding of the factors influencing the development of the Ibaloi property system.

In my research, I took the dispute-case-history approach to the study of law. This approach is common to Anglo-American legal anthropology, but I did not select it beforehand. It emerged as a consequence of the way informants responded to questions about who had rights to which resources. In order to demonstrate their difficulty in answering such questions, informants always reverted to descriptions of key disputes involving resources. In this way they were better able to demonstrate that access to resources depended on how you interpreted your rights and subsequently pressed your claim. How rights were interpreted, in turn, depended on the selective appropriation of normative concepts. Finally, the normative concepts relied on were determined by the best chance of upholding property rights against the competition.

Examining this relationship between law, property systems, kinship and individual purposive strategies raised certain questions regarding anthropological theory which are not new. Specifically, the Ibaloi research results did not fit well with established kinship and property-system approaches. Struggling with this discrepancy led to a critical evaluation of those approaches (*cf.* Schneider 1984). My research results support Goody's (1990) argument that the West has "primitivized" much of "the Rest," but in this book I extend Goody's argument to include property systems and law as well as kinship. While Goody focusses on primitivization, this work focusses on *simplism,* as a consequence of the ''West/the Rest'' contrast.

My research was conducted during a period of considerable upheaval in Philippine society. The assassination of the opposition leader, Benigno Aquino, in August 1983 created marked civil unrest and sharp economic fluctuations. Suspicion of foreigners ran high. Many Filipinos considered their internal political and economic problems a result of interference by external, primarily American, agencies. All foreigners were suspected of being ''Americanos,'' whatever their professed nationality. Nevertheless, many people we met were helpful, considerate and interested in the research. During the first months of field work, we lived in Baguio City and I did research at the Cordillera Studies Center. After we took up residence in the village of Kabayan, our friends and the facilities in Baguio City regularly provided my husband and me with a haven from the rather intense experience of being the only resident foreigners in a small, mountain community.

Kabayan Poblacion was selected as the research site because it met all the research design requirements. From a practical perspective, the community also had several advantages. Community officials and elders were receptive to the idea of having research done in Kabayan, and it was possible to rent accommodation. Accessible by Cordilleran standards, travel to Kabayan via the National Road was always exciting, frightening and boring in succession. The National Road is a single-lane dirt track, often closed during the rainy season by slides. Switchbacks, poor road conditions and weather often combine to make the trip from Baguio City last over five hours despite the distance being less than 90 kilometres. Nevertheless, normally there is a daily bus from Baguio City, which stops on request to pick up or drop off passengers, produce, livestock, household goods and merchandise for *sari sari* (general goods) stores along the route. Numerous jeepnies also ply this road, carrying passengers and cargo at a slightly lower fare than the bus, but with a higher rate of discomfort and danger. Since Kabayan is the administrative and business centre for the municipality, there is a great deal of travel in and out of the community. Kabayan supports a post office, municipal offices, elementary and high schools, a hotel, a market and even a museum and youth hostel (which were still "under construction" during our stay—although we never saw anyone working on the half-completed buildings). There is also a farmer's credit union and farm supply store. All of this contributed to a more ready acceptance of our presence, although we still faced curiosity and suspicion regarding our true purpose there. There were fears that we were going to pot hunt in local mummy caves, to find the motherlode of the numerous small native mines or seek the legendary lost treasure of the Japanese wartime general, Yamashita. Despite the persistence of such rumours, we were able to do our research with few problems.

The research methodology employed an anthropological community case-study approach. We first conducted a total census of the community households using a pre-designed census form. This established a base-line body of information on the individual members, economic resources and socio-economic interconnections of these households. For awhile we considered much of this data suspect because of people's initial reaction to our presence in Kabayan. We were to discover, however, that from the beginning the people were surprisingly candid with us, although they were not above using our ignorance to avoid giving us information. We next mapped the physical layout of the community, including residences, major field sections and the irrigation canals. Interviewing followed, covering numerous topic areas, including history, property relations and disputes, kinship, agricultural practices, irrigation organization, commercial production, religion and external influences. A cohort analysis (Rosaldo 1980) provided an emic historical time frame. Several key informants emerged and provided genealogical information as well as taking us to participate in and observe events such as weddings, *tong tong* (customary courts), *cañaos* (ritual feasts), gold mining and panning, outings to the mummy caves and fishing. An economic survey of a smaller sample of households along a single irrigation system provided more detailed information on a number of topics, including labour allocations and involvement in gold panning. We began another total household survey just before leaving the community, which was designed to document changes occurring during the research period and to take advantage of our fuller understanding of many issues.

For information on how Kabayan differed from or resembled other areas of the Cordillera, other researchers were consulted throughout the study period, especially those affiliated with the Cordillera Studies Center at U.P. Baguio. It must be pointed out that the data on which this monograph is based refer only to Kabayan Poblacion, except where specifically contrasted against other communities. Other Ibaloi communities vary widely in their socio-economic characteristics (see, for example, Russell 1983).

Many Ibaloi must be credited with their assistance on this project. The people of Kabayan Poblacion put up with questions which, when they were not repetitive and dull-witted, must have seemed impertinent. Without their thoughtful and well-considered replies, this monograph could not have been written. The efforts of my research assistants, Jane Mendoza, Jackie Delfin and Estrella Tampoc are very much appreciated. A special vote of thanks also goes to Victoria and Veloso Delfin, George Merino, Bernardo Sinong, Marcelino Alumno, Barangay Captain Galmote and Benid Palmer. Many other residents of the community, local bureaucrats and university students also made welcome contributions. I would especially like to thank the staff and members of the Cordillera Studies Center, including the former director, Benjamin Abellera, for all of their assistance. I also benefitted from discussions with other anthropologists, both in Canada and in the Philippines, including George Appell, Don Reid, Inge Bolin, June Prill-Brett, Susan Russell and Henry T. Lewis. Financial support was provided by a doctoral fellowship from the Social Sciences and Humanities Research Council of Canada, and by a dissertation fellowship from the University of Alberta. During my stay in the Philippines, research affiliation was with the Philippine Institute of Culture, Ateneo de Manila University. This book has been published with the help of a grant from the Canadian Federation for the Humanities, using funds provided by the Social Sciences and Humanities Research Council of Canada.

Finally, I would like to express my heartfelt gratitude to my "companion," Darcy J. Dignam, for his constant support, interest, criticisms, valuable assistance in the field, at the computer terminal and at the drafting table. May he always "accompany" me in my travels. This monograph is dedicated to him.

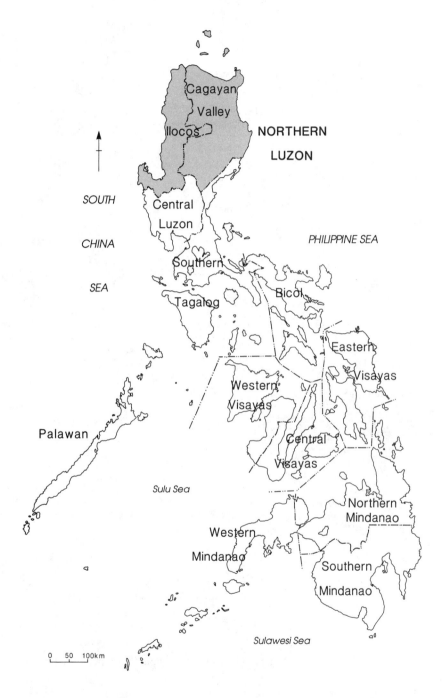

Map 1. The Philippines with Northern Luzon Indicated.

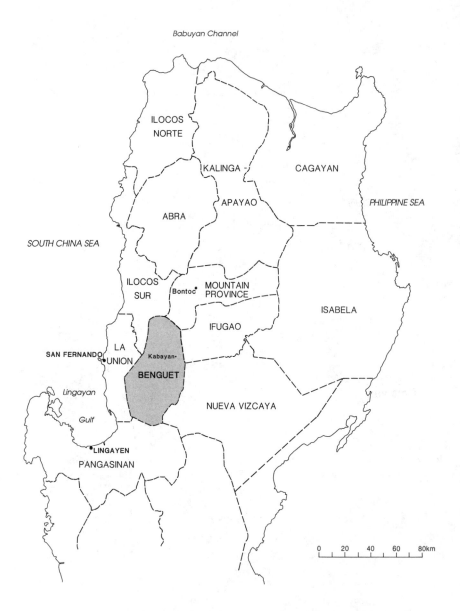

Map 2. The Provinces of Northern Luzon with Benguet Province Indicated.

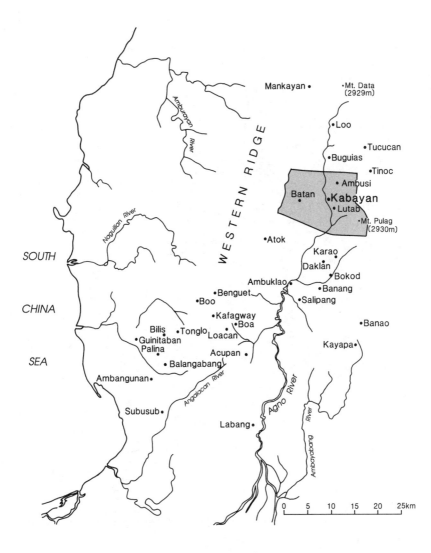

Map 3. The Benguet Area in the Eighteenth Century Showing Major Settlements and with the Modern Boundaries of Kabayan Muncipality Indicated.

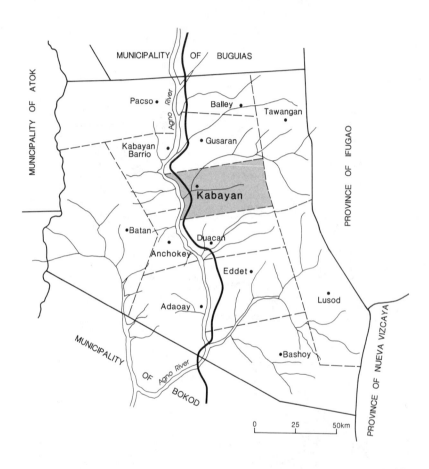

Map 4. The Barangays of the Municipality of Kabayan with Kabayan Poblacion Indicated.

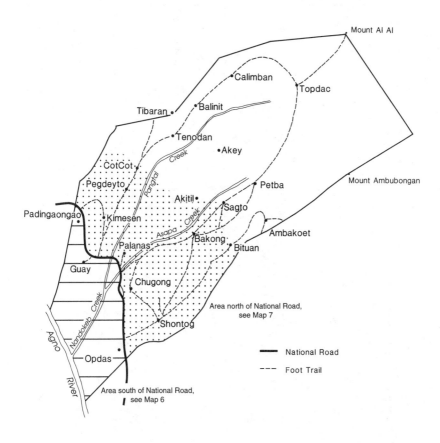

Map 5. The Main Sitios of Kabayan Poblacion with Kabayan Poblacion Central Indicated.

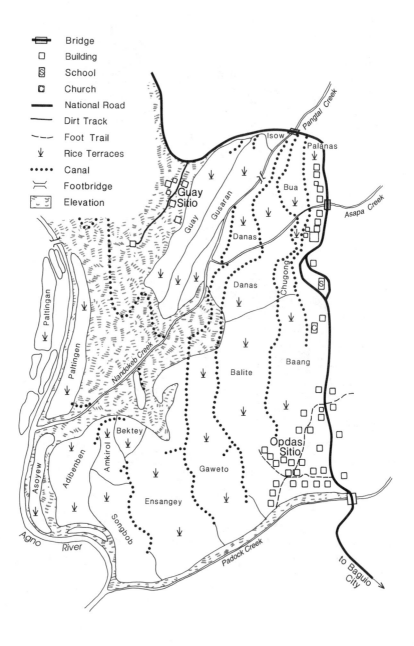

Legend:

- Bridge
- Building
- School
- Church
- National Road
- Dirt Track
- Foot Trail
- Rice Terraces
- Canal
- Footbridge
- Elevation

Map labels: Pangial Creek, Isow, Palanas, Guay Sitio, Guay, Gusaran, Bua, Asapa Creek, Danas, Chugong, Danas, Paltingan, Paltingen, Nandokeb Creek, Balite, Baang, Bektey, Amkirol, Adibenben, Gaweto, Opdas Sitio, Asoyew, Songbob, Ensangey, Agno River, Padock Creek, to Baguio City

Map 6. Kabayan Poblacion Central below the National Road Showing Major Canals and Terraces.

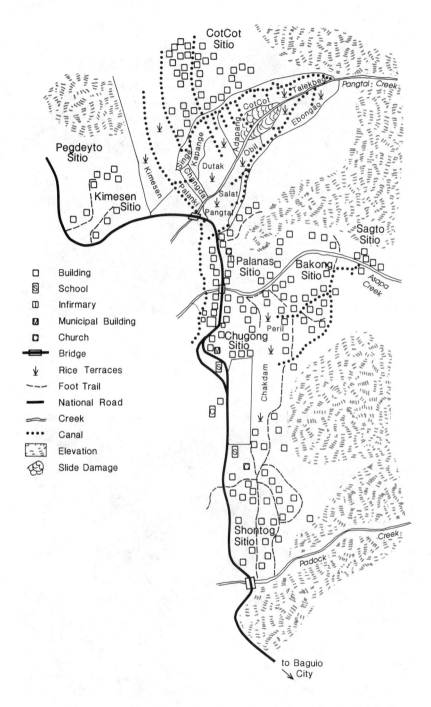

CotCot
Sitio

Pangtal: Creek

Talekbed

CotCot

Ebongao

Adapang

Obil

Kapange

Singa

Chanada

Dutak

Pegdeyto
Sitio

Kimesen

Palank

Salat

Pangtal

Kimesen
Sitio

Sagto
Sitio

Palanas
Sitio

Bakong
Sitio

Asapa
Creek

Peril

Chugong
Sitio

Chakdam

Shontog
Sitio

Padock

Creek

to Baguio
City

□	Building
Ⓢ	School
⊞	Infirmary
Ⓜ	Municipal Building
◙	Church
⊟	Bridge
↓	Rice Terraces
---	Foot Trail
▬	National Road
≈	Creek
••••	Canal
⬚	Elevation
⬡	Slide Damage

Map 7. Kabayan Poblacion Central above the National Road with Irrigation and Terrace Layout Indicated.

Plate 1. Kabayan Poblacion Central viewed from the west.

Plate 2. Land preparation at the beginning of the dry season.

Plate 3. Entrance to abandoned mine shaft.

Plate 4. Meat preparation prior to distribution at a cañao.

Plate 5. The author participating in cañao tayaw (dance).

ONE
Setting the Stage

Introduction

At the turn of the last century, Claude Moss, an American school teacher, lived and worked with the Ibaloi people of Kabayan Barrio in the mountains of the northern Philippines. Eighty years later, when I came to Kabayan Poblacion to investigate the irrigation system, a copy of the work produced by Moss (1919), entitled: "Nabaloi Law and Ritual," was kept in the town hall. As one of the few published works available on the Ibaloi, I had read Moss before coming to the Philippines. With my interest in irrigation, I needed to know how people gained access to water and to irrigated land; land tenure and property rights in general followed as important topics. Soon after arriving in the community, however, it became apparent that Moss's work was not reliable for information on these questions. I found various contradictory normative concepts being employed in Ibaloi[1] property allocations;[2] some of these concepts resembled those identified by Moss, but many others were quite different. The Ibaloi property system had undergone a transformation. As my research evolved, I realized that it continued the work of Claude Moss by documenting the effects of subsequent years of social and political change on Ibaloi property law.

---

1 See Scheerer (1905) for a discussion of the Ibaloi dialect (called Nabaloi) and the difficulties of translating it into written English form. To complicate matters, many Ibaloi terms are borrowed from Spanish, Ilocano and American sources. In addition, word meanings have changed since Scheerer's time. Consequently, spelling and use of these words reflects the usage in Kabayan during the research period. See the Glossary for current meanings.
2 Contradiction existed even in Moss's day; several times his informants complained: "Now there is the law of the Americans." Especially in the area of corporal punishment, the Ibaloi were no longer free to follow their customary law (see Moss 1919:239).

In sequential fashion, the research expanded as a number of topics became important to understanding this jural transformation. My first concern was to investigate how diachronic processes had affected the Ibaloi property system in regards to three resources: land, water and gold. I found first, that the role of group ownership (corporate, communal) of such resources in Ibaloi society was inconsistent with theoretical expectations about cognatic societies. This suggested that I needed to better understand the impact of political incorporation and economic integration on the Ibaloi property system; leading, in turn, to questions about the operation of legal pluralism. Then I became interested in the relationship between the above changes in normative structure and the individual economic strategies which apparently emerged out of, utilized, and sustained legal pluralism. Variation in the patterns of individual strategies led to an interest in the relationship of these strategies to social stratification. Given my original interest in rural development, I began to suspect that the impact of all of the above on development programs (and vice versa) had been underrated. Finally, I began to examine what the Ibaloi situation suggested for anthropological methodology and theory in the comparative study of property systems. These topics are explored in some detail in this monograph.

In this chapter, I begin with some stage-setting. I provide a brief theoretical backdrop through a discussion of recent developments in the field of legal anthropology, specifically legal pluralism. I then place the Ibaloi in the larger geo-political environment of the Philippines, followed by a description of the research community, and finally, of general Kabayan household characteristics. I conclude this stage-setting chapter with an outline of the organization of the book.

An analysis of the Ibaloi situation suggests that the key to understanding the relationship between the several topics addressed in this book lies within the concept of legal pluralism. This term has been used to refer to a situation where more than one body of law is found to co-exist, each competing for the loyalty of a group of people (see Pospisil 1967, 1971, Moore 1978, Merry 1988). As a juristic phenomenon in many non-Western societies, legal pluralism is often explained by reference to Andre Gunder Frank's (1969) dependency theory. Peripheral zones are politically incorporated under the powers of a central zone, and law is one tool enabling members of the centre to accomplish this (see Burman and Harrell-Bond 1979). Imposition of an "alien law" is considered as the first step in the eventual loss of political autonomy and economic self-sufficiency; the process of political incorporation is viewed as inexorably tied to the process of economic integration (see Lopez-Gonzaga 1983:3). Once jurisdiction over resources is established under new legal codes, economic benefits are drained off, creating underdevelopment in the peripheral zones. This explanation offers some clue to the situation faced by the Ibaloi; as with other minority groups, the Philippine government has long viewed the best fate for the Ibaloi as one of integration into the national social, economic and political structures of the larger society. Resources found within Ibaloi territory are viewed as national resources and Ibaloi access to them has been continually challenged. Along with other minority groups, the Ibaloi have struggled for several centuries to contain the impact of such policies. The Spanish and the American colonial periods were significant times of change for the Ibaloi. And yet, as this research demonstrates, dependency theory and the idea that external forces create implacable changes over which local people have no control, can be challenged (see also James Scott 1985).

To understand the dynamics of behaviour in present-day Kabayan, one can rely on neither assumptions of conservative traditionalism nor of rapid social, economic and political change through domination. The community proved to be a surprise in many respects. Behavioural norms in the community appear to exist at two distinct levels, especially in relation to the jural system; a fact often misinterpreted by government bureaucrats. Further, as this monograph will demonstrate, individuals within Ibaloi culture have often been able to manipulate the discrepancy between the two normative levels to their own advantage, and to do so in ways that are innovative or creative. Individual economic strategies have meant that both normative levels are changing, each being affected by the other. It is becoming increasingly obvious that this is a pattern common to many minority groups in developing nations (see, for example, Moore 1986) and in developed nations as well. This suggests that the juristic approach to legal pluralism may be too narrow. Another, broader approach has focussed in recent years on the "social science" view of legal pluralism (see Griffiths 1986).

Stimulated by Pospisil's work (1967, 1971), the "social science" approach suggests that the processes which give rise to legal pluralism are found in every heterogeneous society. The use of this focus allows for the challenge of a number of assumptions about law, property control and the role of individual strategies in the economic integration of the so-called "peripheral" regions of the globe. Following Norman Long's (1986:13) work, this book supports the idea that individual regions experience different and individual processes of political incorporation and of economic integration. These processes, in turn, give rise to subordinate groups who compete with dominant groups for economic and political advantage. The social structural consequences are system-wide. This can better be explained if it is understood that certain kinds of political incorporation everywhere lead to legal pluralism, and this, in turn, offers certain kinds of opportunities to men and women of all nations as they struggle to control resources necessary for economic survival. Since law is one mechanism by which property rights are defined, manipulation of law is a significant process in the economics of all societies. As law is manipulated, it changes; since *all* competing levels of law change under economic and political influences, it is instructive to look at the feedback relationship among politics, economics and law. The ongoing experiences of the Ibaloi people are instructive for a wider understanding of processes that affect us all. This analysis suggests new questions and research directions regarding economic and political stratification, property rights and control, economic and ritual intensification and political centralization.

The Ibaloi

The Republic of the Philippines is approximately 72 000 square kilometres in area with a population in excess of 57 million people, most of whom reside on eight main islands (see Map 1). While these islands are largely mountainous, the majority of the population are found on the coastal plains. Until recently, the interior mountain regions have been sparsely populated by a number of minority groups. Luzon, the largest island, contains some of the most rugged mountains, including the Sierra Madre and the Cordillera Central. The latter is an extensive upland area of 24 000 square kilometres which covers much of the northern half of Luzon Island, moderating as it advances northward. The highest peaks, source of several major river systems, are found in the southern end of the range. As in other areas of the Philippines, the development of forestry, mineral resources and hydroelectric facilities has increasingly brought the national government of the lowlands majority into conflict with the minority groups of this region, collectively known as the Igorot.

Six provinces cover the Cordillera heights, including Benguet, Nueva Viscaya, Ifugao, Mountain Province, Abra and Kalinga-Apayao (see Map 2). Some of the Igorot occupying these provinces are known internationally because the national government promotes their mountain rice terraces as tourist attractions; locations such as Banawe in Mountain Province are visited annually by thousands of foreigners. Further, many Igorot societies such as the Bontoc, the Ifugao and the Kalinga have been studied by American ethnographers since the turn of the last century. This work documents the religion and rituals, folk law, kinship systems and agricultural production methods of these people (see, for example, Barton 1949 and 1969, Conklin 1980, Dozier 1967, Jenks 1905, Keesing and Keesing 1934). However, the Igorot of the province of Benguet are an exception. Despite, or perhaps because of, being the earliest to have regular contact with Western cultures, beginning with the Spanish in 1571, the Benguet Igorot are the least studied of the minority groups of the Cordillera Central.

The Spanish arrived in northern Luzon in the sixteenth century, following the trail of gold and slave-bearing Chinese trade junks. Pushing into the Cordillera Central, they ran into the fierce resistance of the Igorot, especially those in the southern region where the gold was said to originate. It was not until the late eighteenth century that the Spanish achieved a permanent military foothold in this area. When the American administration replaced the Spanish colonial government in 1898, the Igorot of the gold-producing region were considered to have been strongly influenced by Spanish contact. This circumstance was used to explain their anomalous, highly stratified society in a region known for fragmented and egalitarian social organization. Ibaloi leaders were wealthy in cattle, gold, slaves and land. Their ritual life was so elaborate that the entire estate of a dead man was often consumed in mortuary ceremonies lasting months. Further, cultural features known to be common to other Igorot groups were absent; headhunting and internecine warfare between neighbouring villages no longer existed. American ethnographers sent to the Cordillera by the Bureau of Non-Christian Tribes rapidly pushed north to study the more "traditional" cultures of the Bontoc and Kalinga. The Ibaloi, known as gold miners and traders, cattle barons and, more recently, mid-latitude commercial vegetable producers, were only examined during the American period by a single school teacher. Even now, very little detail fills in the broad generalized picture of an Hispanicized uplands people, acculturated to Western ways, and struggling to come to grips with new economic realities such as the American takeover of their gold mines and the more recent invasions of their pasture and croplands by lowlands Filipinos (see Tapang 1985).

As historians, anthropologists and economists begin to take a closer look at the Ibaloi, however, it is obvious that there were far too many assumptions made about the nature of their culture and its diachronic developments in the period following the Spanish arrival. There is still a tendency to interpret Ibaloi culture as a result of Western societies impinging on and changing the Ibaloi, usually for the worse. This book examines the Ibaloi property system and demonstrates that the changes which took place were complex and had numerous directions and relationships, many of them steered by the nature of Ibaloi society itself, others by the Spanish and still others by the resources and environment of Benguet Province. While the study was originally designed to examine the organization of Ibaloi irrigation, it rapidly became obvious that no one aspect of the property system could be understood without an appreciation of the whole. Understanding the Ibaloi property system rapidly became an exercise in diachronic research on social stratification, ritual and law.

The Setting

Located in the southern end of the Cordillera Central, Benguet Province (see Map 2) is characterized by rugged terrain, including Mount Pulag, the highest peak in the Cordillera. This is the sacred source of origin for the Ibaloi people and the final home in the afterlife for the ancestors. The province is bisected by the valley of the Agno River, the floor of which has a gently rolling terrain. Here the climate is more temperate than the hot lowlands, but warmer than the heights above it. The area has two distinct seasons: the dry, from November to April, and the wet, from May to November, with frequent typhoons during September and October. Precipitation ranges from 175 to 500 centimetres per year, with maximum rainfall occurring between June and September. The dominant vegetation in Benguet is pine trees (*Pinus insularis*) interspersed with broad expanses of cogon grasses (*Imperata spp.*). Agricultural cultivation is found between 300 metres above sea level on the valley floors to over 1700 metres on the grassy mountain sides. Agricultural fields are traditionally of two types: irrigated rice paddies and vegetable gardens on the lower slopes and dryland gardens of root crops and other vegetables grown during the wet season at higher elevations.

Benguet is primarily rural; Baguio City dominates the province as the only major urban centre. Its large and untidy sprawl was originally stimulated by an American military rest camp and then by the mining industry, agribusiness development and transportation. Designated summer capital of the Philippines, its mountain setting attracts government bureaucrats as well as foreign tourists. A number of visitors to the area travel on the local bus lines up the historic Mountain Trail to the popular Banawe rice terraces to the north. Fewer people follow the National Road north-east, up over the Ambuklao hydroelectric dam and deeper into the Agno River system to the mummy burial cave sites of Kabayan Municipality and Mount Pulag (see Map 4). Kabayan Poblacion is the last stop on the National Road, which ends at a turn-around loop a few kilometres past it. This area is known as the "cultural heartland" of the Ibaloi peoples.

Kabayan Poblacion (see Map 5) comprises a number of *sitios* (hamlets or neighbourhoods). All Ibaloi communities are characterized by a scattered settlement pattern of numerous *sitios*, except where the government has installed services such as a road or electricity, resulting in more dense residential clusters. The six largest *sitios* of Kabayan Poblacion all hug the National Road and are collectively known as Kabayan Central. Smaller *sitios* with widely dispersed houses are found higher up the slopes of the surrounding mountains. Kabayan Central sits with its back against the flanks of Mount Al-Al and Mount Ambobongan and lies in the middle of extensive rice terraces which flow away from the houses and down the mountainside to the

Agno River (see Map 6). These rice terraces are central to the agricultural system of the Kabayan Ibaloi; although they grow dryland crops on the slopes above, they feel that rice production sets them apart from the *kadasan* or "hillbillies" who only grow swidden fields of sweet potatoes. Kabayan farmers are rice and root-crop producers who may or may not be involved in a marginal production of market vegetables. There is some livestock production (mainly pigs and chickens) but this is generally for home consumption. Two annual rice crops (*Oryza sativa*) are supplemented by rice supplies imported from the lowlands. Camote (*Ipomoea batatas*), a traditional staple before rice was introduced and still an important component in the diet, is a sweet potato grown in dry gardens. Another traditional staple, taro or gabi (*Colocasia esculenta*), is grown in wet areas.

Terraced rice paddies descend over two kilometres to the river banks below. The paddies are narrow for the most part, and in some places the retaining walls between terraces are over eight feet tall. Kabayan has an extensive irrigation network which supplies the terraced landscape (see Maps 6 and 7). On my first day in the community, the mayor told me that irrigation was the "life's blood" of the people there. Without irrigation, rice could not be grown during the highly productive dry season. My original interest was in the co-operative effort and shared patterns of resource ownership that were required to build, maintain and manage an irrigation system in such terrain. I was also interested in what effect the introduction of cash-cropping of mid-latitude vegetables was having on a formerly "subsistence" production regime. The community was recommended by university people from Baguio City as a conservative community, not only in language use but also in land-tenure patterns and in agricultural production. However, the people were said to be experimenting with cash-cropping on a limited basis. Also, Kabayan Central is almost exclusively Ibaloi; unlike many other communities in Benguet, it does not have a large component of recent immigrant groups from the lowlands.

As an administrative unit, Kabayan Poblacion is the central settlement of the large municipality of Kabayan. It was created by the American administration when it located municipal offices and schools in the old barangay (town) of Lutab in 1900. Thereafter, the old barangay of Kabayan, a few kilometres away, became known as Kabayan Barrio, while Lutab became Kabayan Poblacion (see Map 3 for historic place names). Both of these settlements had existed long before the American regime. In 1788, Kabayan was a settlement of 37 households; it had grown to 106 households by 1839. In 1898, the Spanish census found 844 residents in "Cabayan" (*Pronouncing Gazeteer* 1902:397,609). Except for a severe decline during the war years (1939-46), the population of the entire municipality has grown steadily. The population in Kabayan Poblacion, on the other hand, has fluctuated over the years, reaching 1337 people in 1970 and subsequently dropping to around 1015 in 1980, according to the Philippine Government census of that year. The base-line census conducted for this research found just under 1000 residents in 184 households in Kabayan Poblacion in 1983-84.

Kabayan Poblacion is a subsistence community in the sense that the majority of household production is consumed in the household. However, it is also integrated into the market economy, since a sizeable proportion of household consumption depends upon supplies purchased from outside markets. Cash is obtained from several sources: the occasional sales of vegetables, gold, a pig or chickens; renting space to teenagers who come to study at the Kabayan high school; receiving remittances from relatives who live and work overseas; operating small-scale *sari sari* stores or other businesses; and finally, the salaries of the lucky few who have permanent employment. Only 41 households rely on farming as their sole source of income; however, 134 households (or 74.7%) gain at least some of their income from farm sources. Other signs of the integration of the community into the national economy are numerous. The majority of homes include galvanized iron and cement in their construction materials. Electricity arrived in the community about a decade ago. Many homes subscribe to the national magazines and newspapers that are sold in the stores. An important index of the relative affluence of the people of Kabayan is the daily sale of meat in the community. For the majority of communities in the Cordillera, meat remains largely a prestige or ritual food and is only consumed on ceremonial occasions.

These signs of economic integration signal deeper transformations in Ibaloi society, many of which have their roots in political incorporation. The historical patterns of response by the Kabayan Ibaloi to external economic and political influences is the central focus of this book. More than an ethnohistory, however, the book documents how diachronic forces have shaped current-day Kabayan society into a system with sharp, built-in discrepancies, especially in the property system. The Ibaloi continue to differ culturally from their lowlands majority neighbours; but more significantly, their path has continued to diverge sharply from that of their mountain neighbours, the Bontok, Ifugao and Kalingas. In the strict hierarchy of their social life, in the special complexities of their ritual systems and in the complex transformations of their economic life, the Ibaloi offer a number of interesting lessons for cultural history and for cultural change. These lessons, in turn, offer suggestions for new directions in the anthropological study of property systems, law and social stratification.

Organization of the Book

This chapter has briefly established the theoretical interests of the book and introduced the cultural and regional setting. Chapter Two provides a more detailed theoretical introduction to the complex, multi-strand analysis conducted herein. It begins with a critique of the simplistic formal models developed for the comparative study of property systems in anthropology and then proceeds to examine an alternative methodological model proposed by George Appell (1974). In this model, Appell attempts to encompass change by recognizing three "levels" of social organization: social structure, opportunity structure and emergent structure. To distinguish among them, he argues, we must recognize the moment of reification when behaviour from the opportunity structure becomes accepted. He argues that this moment of reification can be identified by reference to indigenous normative orders such as the jural system. While Appell's model proved useful in my research, there were some problems springing from Appell's failure to recognize legal pluralism as an empirical fact. The chapter concludes with a discussion of the relationship between property and law, the complexities of which are better understood as a result of recent work in the field of legal pluralism.

Thus Chapter Two provides a theoretical springboard for the discussion of the Ibaloi which follows. Chapter Three begins with the historical background to present-day Ibaloi society. It follows the Ibaloi from their first appearance in historical documents of the Spanish (*c.* 1591) to the end of the American administration after World War II. This history falls logically into four periods. In the first period, from 1591 to 1624, the Ibaloi are characterized as fiercely resistant to Spanish incursions into their territory. Nevertheless, here appears the first outline of the subsequent patterns of accommodation to the Spanish presence in the lowlands. Culture heros emerge through resolving the twin problems created by the Spanish, including the military incursions after the source of upland gold and the upheavals in Cordilleran political relationships that these forays create. In the second period (1754-1800), the Ibaloi patterns of accommodation become entrenched, including increased social stratification and control by the elite of the most important productive resources: gold, cattle and labour. By the third period (1800-1900), the Ibaloi elite have become so successful as traders of cattle and contraband gold and tobacco that the colonial government is forced to finance a military reduction of the region to end this drain on Spanish trade monopoly income. While the consequence is a period of incredible destruction for Ibaloi villages and agriculture, the Ibaloi elite manage not only to survive, but to also emerge as valued collaborators in the fragile Spanish military control of Benguet.

This collaboration was probably inspired by entrepreneurial practicalities. The elite retained many economic advantages under the Spanish administration, a situation which continued to a certain extent in the final historical period discussed. This period began at the turn of the century and lasted until approximately 1945. Although the Spanish were ousted by the combined efforts of Filipino insurrectionists and American expeditionary forces, the promised Philippine independence did not materialize. During the American Administration, the Cordillera got the first taste of effective political incorporation, including the encroachment onto elite lands and mines by American opportunists under American colonial laws. The advantaged position of the elite did not finally decline, however, until the upheavals created by the Japanese invasion during World War II.

Chapter Four is a diverse ethnographic account of the people of Kabayan. In Appell's terms, this account includes not only the social structure (religion, politics, kinship and economy) but also some aspects of the opportunity structure which in large part is a result of conditions generated by political incorporation and economic integration. This material is important and necessary background for the following discussion in Chapter Five of several significant disputes over property in Kabayan. Material in Chapter Four allows the reader to make sense of individual strategies pursued in these property disputes; such strategies involve the appropriation of normative concepts from several different sources as well as their manipulation in the community context.

Nowhere is the impact of legal pluralism more apparent than in the current chaos surrounding issues of property rights. Those individuals and social groups which clearly existed as property-holding entities in the past are currently being redefined in the context of modern political conditions. The process of redefinition is exposed in the informant accounts of key historic disputes and in the differing interpretation of the outcome of these disputes offered by members of the community. It is at this level of gossip and interpretation that law enters into the life of a community, and not in the actual decisions rendered and documented in court procedures. For this reason, the emphasis in Chapter Five is on the knowledge of disputes available to and current among community members. Similarly, Chapter Six documents the current and uneasy emergent structures in Kabayan by addressing the following questions: what social entities are currently gaining access to property in Kabayan and how are they justifying their claims? How are their arguments viewed by other members of the community?

Chapter Seven is an analysis of those processes by which Ibaloi institutions were transformed. Several significant variables are discussed for their influence on these processes, including: the role of competing jural authorities; the rise of economic stratification which promoted individual manipulation of the discrepancy between these jural orders; and finally, the patterns of manipulation followed by the competing socio-political strata in Ibaloi society. This chapter also raises the issue of the recent promotion of the concept of customary communalism by Cordillerans in their strategy to regain control of local resources and the uses to which they are put. This "invention" of custom is consistent with the findings of other researchers in the field of legal pluralism.

The concluding chapter places my findings on the broader stage of anthropological theory and methodology. It raises the issue of the relationship between structure and process in human societies and shows how law is one area of social life in which an understanding of this relationship is vital. "Emergent structuralism," in Appell's terms, is the stuff of which normative debate is made. This book demonstrates that conflict over resources is often couched, not in terms of normative expectations, but in terms of what the market will bear. Innovation is a strategy that can be employed by any player, and the impact on the game is frequently unforeseen. The consequences set up the next round of negotiations in which emergent structure becomes the force to be reckoned with. If, as the recent literature on legal pluralism suggests, this pattern holds true for most societies, then anthropology will have to seriously reconsider many basic concepts in the comparative analysis of property and law.

TWO

"Primitive" Property Systems: Theoretical Issues

In her book on the Chagga of Kilimanjaro, Sally Falk Moore (1986:38) asks the question: "How rule-bound were the Chagga?" Similar questions now dominate many fields of anthropology, including kinship and law. How rule-bound are members of any human society? New research suggests that old notions of rule-governed behaviour need re-examination, as do the theoretical models on which they rest. This chapter is concerned with this question and explores it by critiquing the long-standing theoretical connection between the normative orders regulating kinship and property control. The chapter argues that this connection is based on a gross simplification of empirical data.

Such oversimplification is probably basic to rule-centred social theory. Goody (1990) has recently complained of it in his critique of the "primitivization" of Asian kinship systems (and their resulting categorization as the same "types" as unilineal African systems). The property systems of non-Western societies have been similarly "primitivized" into two ideal types: communal societies practising bilateral kinship and corporate societies practising unilineal descent. This formal model-oriented view has dominated the analysis of non-Western property systems to the detriment of our theory and understanding. Recent research has tackled the empirical question of the relationship between property control and kinship. This chapter critically examines one such alternative model which relies on indigenous law to sort out rights to property and the social entities which hold them. The chapter concludes by suggesting that the Ibaloi data presents problems for this alternative approach; again, the concern is with oversimplification of non-Western societies.

This book deals with property systems, by which I refer to two linked phenomena. In my view, property systems are both structure and process; that is, both a normative set of expected behaviours and the actual behaviours pertaining to or coming out of the expectations (see Giddons 1984 and Comaroff and Roberts 1981 on structure and process). In terms of property systems, the structure aspect may be identified as including resources, or more properly, the uses to which resources are, or can be, put; social entities with an interest in those resources, which Appell (1976) has called "right and duty bearing units"; and rules regarding the expected relationship between resources and social entities.[1] The process aspect of property systems includes production, dispute, devolution, alienation and other behavioural processes affecting property and the uses to which social entities can and do put property. The relationship between structure and process has always been a problematic one in anthropology and is no less so in this analysis. As structure, property systems are intertwined with other societal structures; for this reason, it has been necessary to incorporate a discussion of religion, kinship and politics as well as of law in this analysis of the Ibaloi property system. To complicate things further, processes which affect property are in themselves affected by these other societal structures and their processes: production by kinship, religion, politics; dispute by law, politics and kinship; inheritance, devolution and alienation by kinship, law, politics and religion. The strands of influence in the dialectical relationship between process and structure are extremely complex. Nonetheless, no analysis of property systems is complete without some cognizance of these complex connections.

With a dialectic focus, the picture is that much more complicated. Ibaloi societal structures have not stood still over time. Individual patterns of behaviour have been informed by and in their turn have affected the structural patterns of Ibaloi life. Two important processes significant for an understanding of past events in Ibaloi culture include the twin mechanisms of political incorporation and economic integration by which external state agencies have attempted to link the peripheral Ibaloi to their larger, centralized structure. Long (1986:15) defines economic integration as "the transformation of subsistence-oriented, non-commoditized forms of household production and exchange, leading to a more commoditized pattern based upon a cycle of reproduction dependent on the functioning of the market and on processes of capital subsumption." To achieve economic integration, central state authori-

---

1   Hallowell (discussed in Bromley 1989:202-203) develops a similar set of three variables with which to "comprehend property relations." Bromley (ibid.:203) reminds us that property is the right(s) and not the object over which rights are extended. Ownership, on the other hand, refers to the bundle of rights held in respect of such an object, and the obligations that those rights instigate. Bromley (ibid.:187) lists the 11 characteristics of full or "liberal" ownership. It is important to remember that limited forms of ownership, in which only a few of these 11 characteristics pertain, are common, especially in non-Western contexts.

ties rely on political incorporation, which is "the process whereby the central government, through the exercise of its legal powers and the mechanisms of bureaucratic coercion, incorporates peripheral communities" (Lopez-Gonzaga 1983:3). As the following discussion will demonstrate, the relationship between the state and peripheral communities in the Philippines has been a struggle to influence individual choice-making. Individuals are confronted with two sets of normative orders (that is, with two sets of structures) but as this study will show, the question has never simply been one of the imposition of and resistance to state law.

Communal, Corporate—Unilineal, Bilateral

When anthropologists study non-Western property relations, two contrasting concepts of rights in property are commonly brought to bear: first, rights lodged at the communal level; and second, rights lodged in kin-based, corporate groups (see Shipton 1984). These two concepts are often correlated with another contrasting set based on kinship: societies practising bilateral or cognatic descent[2] and those practising some form of unilineal descent. It is argued that unilineal descent creates cohesive, corporate groups while bilateral kinship is tied to communal property systems. These two contrasting sets, and their correlation, have been generated by a historical tendency to contrast non-Western examples with the Western pattern of property control which is characterized by individualism (see Grossi 1981). In this separation of West and "non-West," both have been oversimplified; the former is characterized by rationalized individualism and the latter by logical opposites of such individualism. The resulting methodological conundrums can hardly be credited; often, the most basic operational principles are neglected. For example, what empirical data supports the use of such concepts?

Dow (1973:906) shows that anthropologists generally use the concept of corporate group to fill one of two needs: to specify folk concepts of the organization of groups (especially those based on kinship), and to specify folk concepts of property control. Wolf (1957) uses the term to describe "closed" peasant communities, by which he refers to the nature of intragroup and intergroup social and economic relations rather than to property control. The roots of the term in comparative sociology can be found with Maine (1901:148-50) who applies it to the historic Roman family. He argues

---

2 Note here that I treat the two terms cognatic and bilateral as referring to separate kinship phenomena. Bilateral kinship systems trace relatives through either or both the maternal and paternal lines, while cognatic refers to a mode of descent-reckoning where all descendants of an apical ancestor/ancestress, through any combination of male or female links, are included.

that the "primal condition of the human race" was "an aggregation of families" and, therefore, that the first human laws dealt with corporate groups (ibid.:122-26). Maine assumes that the primal family was patriarchal, a social entity with assumed perpetuity, and a property-holding unit. He writes "we can hardly form a notion of the primitive family group unless we suppose that its members brought their earnings of all kinds into the common stock, while they were unable to bind it by improvident individual engagements" (1940:141). In consequence of the responsibilities of the individual towards the family, and of the family towards the individual, Maine (ibid.:145) points out that some jurists considered the Roman parent and child as a "unity of persons" under the law. Finally, Maine (ibid.:148-50) also argues that for the Romans, and presumably for all ancient societies, kinship terminated where females appeared in the family tree, since corporate kinship units could not be subject to two paternal authorities. Thus, corporate groups were not only kinship units, but specifically, kinship units based on unilineal descent; this has proven a very persistent theme in social anthropology. It should also be noted that Maine began the tendency to seek legitimacy of access to property in formal law.

Radcliffe-Brown has consolidated the corporate approach. He (1950:41) writes:

> A group may be spoken of as "corporate" when it possesses any one of a certain number of characteristics: if its members or its adult male members, or a considerable proportion of them, come together occasionally to carry out some collective action—for example, the performance of rights; if it has a chief or council who are regarded as acting as representatives of the group as a whole; if it possesses or controls property which is collective, as when a clan or lineage is a land-owning group.

Although he discusses the ethnographic evidence for non-kin-based, corporate village groups, Radcliffe-Brown (ibid.:42-43) goes on to argue that only "unilineal reckoning makes it possible to create corporate kin groups having continuity in time extending beyond the life of an individual or family." The main concern of the structuralist school is social cohesion and stability over time, and the role of kinship in promoting these (Schneider 1984:45). For example, Radcliffe-Brown dismisses non-kin-based corporate villages as "based on the persons who attach themselves to a headman" (1950:42), while bilateral kinship is viewed as incapable of creating "distinct separate groups, each with its own solidarity, each person belonging to one group of any set" (ibid.:43).

There are some dissenting voices. Of those who focus on non-kin-based corporate groups, the predominant guideline is Wolf's (1957) analysis of corporate peasant communities. Leaning on Weberian sociology, Wolf sees closed corporate peasant communities as arising from "dualized" societies where a "dominant entrepreneurial sector" is opposed to a "dominated sector of native peasants" (1957:8). Others develop this idea further (see Rambo 1973, Behar 1984) but have never seriously challenged the rule that corporate ownership of property is best demonstrated in societies with unilineal descent (see Befu and Plotnicov 1962). Research in bilateral or cognatic societies is also marked by the Radcliffe-Brown straw-man of social order, that is, by the notion that in "primitive" societies, order is kin-based. Appell (1976:5) notes that Radcliffe-Brown introduces the notion that bilateral societies are loosely organized and lack definite structure—probably because of the "lack of an unambiguous method for assigning individuals to social statuses."

There are several problems with this view: it underestimates the organizational ability of members of cognatic societies, and overestimates the "tidiness" of unilineal descent systems (see Goody 1983, 1990). Further, it ignores altogether the importance of other factors such as locality or common purpose in the formation of formal groups (see Shipton 1984). The Western bias that presumes problems with social cohesion and order is at the root of theoretical difficulties with bilateral social organization. When the various publications of Murdock (1960, 1964) and Goodenough (1955, 1961) are examined, for example, one point of debate in reference to bilateral societies is whether or not sufficiently discrete units can be created to serve as the basis for corporate group formation. The argument is that the kinship rules of recruitment create overlapping groups without clear boundaries, and without clear rules for assigning status within the group. Murdock (1960:4) defined a corporate group as "an estate comprising rights over persons and various forms of real, movable, and incorporeal property in whose assets a number of individuals share in accordance with their respective statuses." In bilateral social systems, Murdock (ibid.:2-3) identifies two important kin-based units: the domestic unit, which is "fully corporate" and the kindred, which is too amorphous to serve as the basis for a corporate group, although he acknowledges that the "stem kindred" could be the exception to this rule (1964:129).

In response, Goodenough (1955, 1961) argues that there is confusion over two distinct organizational forms based on kinship: the ego-centred group and the ancestor-oriented group. He argues that the "polar distinction" between unilineal and bilateral descent systems is masking the true distinction, which is one of lateral or radial organization versus lineal organization, both of which can occur in the same society. So-called "non-unilineal" descent groups can form where principles of descent inclusion are other than unilineal (1961:1343). Further, lineally organized groups can be exclusive with restricted membership or they can be unrestricted. Since non-unilineal restricted descent groups have much in common with unilineal ones, he proposes calling both of these forms "lineages" but notes that Murdock prefers the term "ramage" (ibid.:1344). Interestingly, Goodenough (1955:75-76) draws on Barton's account of the Philippine Ifugao to illustrate the existence of non-unilineal descent groups. Subsequent research in bilateral (or cognatic) societies fuels the debate which continues to focus on the corporate nature (or lack thereof) of the non-unilineal descent group (see, for example, Davenport 1959, Eggan 1967, Ember 1959, Firth 1957, Gilbert 1981, Noricks 1983, Scheffler 1964).

The question of corporate organization itself fuels debate in anthropology (see Cochraine's exchange with Goodenough in *American Anthropologist* 1971). When the concept is applied to ethnographic examples of group organization and tenure in property, there is little consensus on definition. Cochraine argues that the concept is applied in two ways, either as "a kind of anthropological colloquialism" or as a term covering distorted ethnographic data. Cochraine writes: "there is evidence to indicate that misunderstanding stemming from use of the corporate concept can obscure the nature of property relations" (1971:1144). The difficulty lies in defining when a corporate group exists; in other words, what are its defining characteristics? For Brown (1974, 1976) who follows Maine (1901) and Smith (1975), a corporate group is an institution with presumed perpetuity. He (1976:40) writes: "the corporate group is characterized by sufficient autonomy, procedures and organization to regulate its exclusive body of common affairs." Such corporate groups develop under appropriate conditions, from various quasi-corporate groups or "corporate categories," which exist in all societies (ibid.:33). This perspective results in some interesting speculation on how the formation of corporate groups from corporate categories might occur and/or be blocked by various forces (see for example, Goodell 1985). For Stoljar (1975:175-77), on the other hand, the essential criterion for a corporate group is the joint ownership of property which is held as a strictly separate legal entity from the social group concerned with it. The members of the group do not merely have a joint interest as in voluntary associations, but a joint ownership which cannot be split up among the individuals involved (ibid.:44). He argues that without the separate legal entity which is the corporation, the corporate group cannot centralize nor distribute liability and property control (ibid.:177).

While the concept of corporate group is often correlated with unilineal descent, the concept of communal group has found wider use with more resulting distortions. In the most rigorous literature, the term communal is used to refer to the lodging of resource rights collectively in a group, membership in which is defined by residence in a common locality. Rights are non-alienable by individuals, are often operationalized by participation in group endeavours and can sometimes be managed and distributed by a group-recognized authority.[3] In the few historical records of European communal systems, such as the Germanic Mark, Maine finds the following characteristics: first, an organized, self-acting suprafamily group, sharing common residence in a community; second, exercising a common proprietorship over a definite tract of land; third, exploiting uncultivated lands (forest, pasture) in its domain on a common system, and fourth, rotating arable lands using a system of lots and regular fallow periods (Grossi 1981:51). In the evolutionary models of Maine's day, collective forms of property-holding and use were viewed as the predecessor to modern property systems. Grossi (1981:23-24) suggests that the nature of this and successive communal concepts originates in the fact that their primary use has been as the inverse of individualism: "the historical and logical *oppositum* of ownership by a single proprietor." In contrast with corporate organization, an interesting feature of such concepts of communalism is the absence of kinship as an organizing factor, a connection later established by Radcliffe-Brown.

When the difficulties of kinship and descent theory are considered together with the problems of defining corporate and communal groups, it is easy to understand why little gain has been made towards understanding property systems in non-Western societies. While anthropologists are expressing increasing discomfort with the above concepts (see Goody 1983: 222-39, Schneider 1984), other problems are generated by the wider public's acceptance of them. Bureaucrats in many nation states maintain that minority groups have unsophisticated methods of property organization which employ communal or corporate structural principles. These property systems are viewed as especially wasteful and destructive under conditions of over-population and the resulting potential for a "tragedy of the commons" (see Wade 1987 for a rejection of this argument). Meanwhile, development agencies attempt to utilize supposedly indigenous patterns of communal organization which may or may not exist (see Dove 1982).

The Philippines are a good example of both these public approaches. While Eggan (1967:188) acknowledges Firth's category of cognatic descent group, he rejects the view that bilateral descent groups are concerned with corporate property control for most uplands people of the northern Philippines (ibid.:195). One exception discussed is the people of Sagada

---

3　In contrast, Appell distinguishes types of property-holding groups based on whether the interest in property is held in severalty rather than collectively. In other words, do individuals form a group merely because they all have individual rights in the same estate, or do they hold rights in an estate as a group, indivisible? He argues that in groups based on rights held in severalty, individual shares are often alienable and devolvable at will.

(ibid.:197). He designates the rather complex systems of affiliation and descent found in the Cordillera as "bilateral." This oversimplification has a corollary in the tendency to discuss uplands property systems in communal terms, despite the excellent documentation of complex patterns of property law by people such as Barton (1949, 1969) and Drucker (1977). The "communalism" of uplands people is entrenched among Philippine bureaucrats in key agencies such as the National Irrigation Authority (see, for example, de los Reyes 1980, de los Reyes et al. 1980, Bagadion and Korten 1980, Cruz, Cornista and Dayan 1987 and Korten and Siy, Jr. 1988), and the now defunct PANAMIN, which was responsible for non-Christian tribal populations (see Lopez-Gonzaga 1983:53). Attempts to "sensitize" state legal institutions have also inappropriately employed the concept (see Aranal-Sereno and Libarios 1983). The failure of the National Irrigation Authority to develop responsible irrigators' associations based on "indigenous communal systems" is a case in point of the peculiar love-hate relationship towards "communalism" which Dove (1982) also documents in Kalimantan.

Despite such problems, anthropologists continue to employ the Western concepts of corporate and communal group to discuss non-Western property systems. Appell (1976:69) rejects this approach. While he recognizes a number of types of social entities which might be termed corporate or communal by Western standards, in his attempt to investigate the question-set dealing with property, he has abandoned the use of Western property-system terms. He argues that these are culturally specific and are impossible to apply to other cultures without the danger of creating "social pseudomorphs," or cultural entities which only exist in the mind of the investigator (Appell 1976:70). Instead, Appell attempts to follow the property question-set approach, and he has produced a method of identifying and defining the empirical phenomenon of property ownership in all its complexity. His methodology was employed in my research and is briefly discussed below.

An Alternative Model?

Appell (1976:vii) argues that it is necessary to trace the creation and devolution of interests in a scarce good back to the individuals or groups concerned with the resource and *only then* concern ourselves with the nature of the recruitment to the group, which is an empirical question to be decided by ethnographic investigation (see Schneider 1984 for a similar conclusion). In his book on the cognatic social structure of Borneo, Appell (1976:67) wrote:

> what I argue here and will attempt to demonstrate with ethnographic materials from the Rungus is that property relations are a universal aspect of all human societies; that social structure is primarily founded on the nature of these relations; and that the question-set dealing with property relations as

a result explains a wider range of phenomena than the question-set that
starts off with an interest in kinship and descent.

Leach (1961:305) writes that what social anthropology calls kinship structure
is actually: "just a way of talking about property relations," especially:
"rights and usages with respect to land" (ibid.:146). Schneider (1984:48)
also views kinship as an idiom: "in terms of which other kinds of social relations and functions are expressed." There is a danger that such materialist
determinism could also oversimplify, but Appell (1974, 1980) resists this
tendency by focussing on what he has termed "emergent structuralism." He
wants to understand how the tension between the social structure and actual
behaviour can create an "opportunity structure." Within the opportunity
structure, social behaviour is tested for acceptance in the social structure.
Members of a society can either recognize new behaviour (a reflexive event
which elevates new behaviour to the social structure) or reject it and thus rel-
egate it to the sphere of deviance. This reflexive event has much to do with
laws, rules and regulations and all the other positive and negative sanctions
which surround and support the social structure (see Appell 1974:2-4; 1976:
67-68; and Arno 1985).

For this reason, Appell focusses on recognition within the indigenous
legal system as the defining characteristic of jural entities or legitimate property-holding units, as opposed to the many other forms of nebulous groups
forming and dissolving in relation to a scarce good. He (1976:68) uses this
principle to distinguish several different types of groups involved in property:

> The jural entity may involve an individual or a social grouping. When a
> social grouping thus holds interests as a jural entity, I refer to it as a *jural
> isolate*, or corporate social grouping. However, when the social grouping
> does not hold the rights as a jural entity, when instead the rights are held
> by the individual members, I refer to this social entity as a *jural aggregate*.
> In certain instances, however, a jural system may recognize the existence
> of social relations between the individual right holders that belong to the
> social grouping and will, as a result, permit one of the members of the
> social grouping to sue on behalf of the other members and equal right
> holders. Such a social grouping which is not a jural isolate, ie. [*sic*] not a
> corporate social grouping, but whose social character is nevertheless rec-
> ognized in the jural system, I refer to as a *jural collectivity* (emphasis
> added).

While I do not employ Appell's terminology in this book, I include this quo-
tation to draw attention to the fact that Appell makes no restrictive definitions
of the membership criteria of these groups, nor their organizational structure.
He is attempting to provide theoretical constructs which "will accommodate
not only the analysis of cognatic social systems but all social systems"
(Appell 1976:67). For my research, it was important to know the Ibaloi con-

ceptions of rights in property and according to Appell, this knowledge had to be based on empirical investigation of their jural order. One of the first methodological hurdles to overcome was a definition of law such that I could establish when a "jural system" existed. This is something which Appell neglects to discuss.

Law and Property: The Nature of the Relationship

Implicit in the aforementioned formal models of communal and corporate, unilineal, cognatic and bilateral is the notion of rule-bound behaviour. However, none of these studies addresses the question of how closely rules govern behaviour, nor how rules are generated in the first place and how the models are affected when compliance is not automatically assumed. Such questions *have* received attention in legal anthropology (see, for example, Moore 1986:38-51), where there are two trends of thought: one has been called the rule-centred approach and the other the process-oriented approach (see Comaroff and Roberts 1981). Central to the rule-centred approach is the notion of an authority which empowers and administers law. For example, Pospisil states: "My concept of law is that it consists of those principles which govern the decisions of the leaders" (Strouthes 1990:9). In contrast, the processual approach is centred on the notion of "self interest" or the utility goals of individual or group action. Here law is an arena of competition (see Collins 1982:17-30). As Comaroff and Roberts (1981:17) point out, the first perspective postulates over-controlled social actors, while the second one has difficulty explaining the necessity of rules.

Comaroff and Roberts (ibid.:19) try to address this impasse by arguing that, however well-enforced by an authority, rules constitute a "loosely structured repertoire rather than an internally consistent code." This only makes sense. Why would we need a dispute-resolution process such as courts if we all knew the rules and followed them? Violations would never be subject to interpretive adjudication but only to investigative processes to establish who perpetrated rule-breaking behaviour. Rules constitute a significant resource for what Appell calls the opportunity structure, in that their breach is always a possibility. Further, since almost all behaviour is subject to competing normative constructions, law is inherently pluralistic. Behaviour remains influenced by rules and structure, but not programmed by it. This fact is both important and difficult. Some researchers, not so absorbed by the question of dispute resolution, have focussed on what has been called the "role of law in a trouble-free social life" (Benda-Beckmann and Strijbosch 1986:6-7). Here case studies of dispute resolution have been dismissed in favour of a wider view of the role of law in socialization and individual orientation in society (see Griffiths 1986 and Holleman 1986).

No aspect of law seems more relevant to both traditions (rules versus process) than property issues, and in property-oriented research, I have not found definitions of law which focus on leadership and the application of authority useful. Since all societies are concerned with questions of property, I also find any definition of law which separates law from social norm and custom and even goes so far as to identify some societies as "without law" too restrictive. Instead, I use F. von Benda-Beckmann's (1983:236-37) approach, which is to view law as:

> cognitive and normative conceptions defining the status of things, persons and relationships, of standards of evaluation, options, prohibitions and other propositions. These are commonly joined in rules or principles, . . . Law thus provides frames of meaning which offer points of orientation for human conduct.

As Moore (1986:42) expresses it: "Law is connected with *ideas about* order, about causality, and about responsibility" (emphasis mine). These ideas have a history and, as with the uses to which property is put, they change over time. Further, no two people hold exactly the same set of ideas about the status of things and people, although one assumes there is significant overlap. Nevertheless, there is also divergence.

In his analysis of 20 years of research on legal pluralism, Vanderlinden (1989) argues that pluralism is ubiquitous in our lives:

> one might say that man [*sic*], as a member of many social networks, is constantly subjected to a dialectical process in which competing regulatory orders assert their power over him [*sic*] and strive to achieve autonomy from the others. Law is one of these regulatory orders and competes with them in order to assert its supremacy at the same time over the individual and over other regulatory orders (ibid.:151).

He goes on to add a most important point:

> When confronted with the reality of competing social networks and hence with rival legal orders, the State system, in order to conceal the inevitable failure of its totalitarian ideal, pretends to incorporate the other legal orders into an order which it calls "legal pluralism." This enables the State system to affirm in principle a monopoly of regulatory order, since it claims that the competing legal orders only exist by virtue of its "toleration" or "recognition" (ibid.:153).

Vanderlinden argues that the only way for scientists to avoid falling prey to such legal centrism is to focus on individuals, since it is individual actors who are involved in networks, experience the contradictory pull of various regulatory orders and decide which shall influence their behaviour (see also Griffiths 1986). While I follow this approach, I go further to demonstrate the combined effects on the property system of individual decisions taken in

Kabayan over the past few centuries. In other words, I examine the relationship between individual choices and emergent structure.

In this book several terms are used in specific ways. On one level, my
book is about legal pluralism in what Griffiths (1986:8) calls the "weak
sense"; that is, the situation established when a hegemonic superordinate
legal order "recognizes" an inferior order and "accommodates it" until a
uniform law can be imposed, as in many post-colonial, non-Western societies. But this book also documents one example of what Griffiths calls the
stronger "descriptive sense" of legal pluralism. Here we are dealing with an
ubiquitous empirical state of affairs: "namely the coexistence within a social
group of legal orders which do not belong to a single system" (ibid.:8). In
this second meaning of legal pluralism, state law is the package of "cognitive
and normative conceptions" which is a factor in individual decision-making
in local arenas, but by definition is supra-local in jurisdiction (in other words,
it has a tendency towards "totalitarianism"). In the Philippines, state law is
built upon various contributing cognitive and normative conceptions, as it is
in all state societies. There are influences from indigenous Southeast Asian,
Spanish and Anglo-American normative orders.

Indigenous law, on the other hand, is used to refer to local traditions
which, although influenced by outside contacts throughout their history, were
until recently part of a "totalitarian ideal" of their own (see Wiber 1989). It
is necessary to keep this point in mind so that indigenous law is not somehow
viewed as inferior or superior to competing normative orders. I reserve the
term customary law to refer to the transformed normative orders which result
in local communities when indigenous law and state law interact over time
(such as the "invented" or "fabricated" law in many recent studies; *cf.*
Bowen 1986, Chanok 1985, Moore 1986). Each of these normative orders has
had an effect on the property-holding social entities identified using Appell's
methodology. The study of property systems and their change over time,
therefore, must take these normative orders into consideration.

But how do we gain information on these multiple normative orders? To
focus exclusively, or even mainly, on law courts and their decisions is to fall
victim to the centrist ideology that what goes on in state institutions is the
real law. Obversely, in the centrist legal ideology, to focus on how people
think and act in relation to *perceived* law is somehow not rigorous research.
Griffiths (1986:12) writes: "Legal pluralism is the name of a social state of
affairs." This book examines a state of social affairs. While Moore (1978,
1986) investigated the effectiveness of state legislation on semi-autonomous
social fields, my book examines behaviour within such a sphere (as an obser-
vational perspective) and shows how differentiated that behaviour is. I am
interested in the effect of that differentiated behaviour on what "the law" is

at any given moment, according to the people who make use of it in their daily purposive strategies.

Only after we have some grasp of the true workings of normative orders can we establish how people are using those normative orders to acquire access to property. The rules of recruitment employed in building the resulting property-holding groups, how the property rights are distributed within them, and finally, how such groups respond to changes in the jural or economic sphere which might affect their property interests are all subjects of empirical investigation which must wait on obtaining that grasp. Only then can we examine the role of kinship in recruitment to corporate groups and the role of corporate or communal organization in the development of productive resources in the local setting.

When Appell's methodology was employed to investigate the property system of the Philippine Ibaloi, his concepts proved useful in identifying social entities involved in property tenure. However, certain problems arose, and these problems were not only concerned with what Brown (1984:813-15) has called a "plurality of jural levels," they also involved the issue of inclusion/exclusion (boundary maintenance) and the diachronic development of property systems. These problems were productive in that they pointed to the above areas as significant theoretical problems which must be addressed if property-system theory is to prove useful in cross-cultural comparisons.

In conclusion, the question of the extent of rule-governed behaviour (of structure) and its relationship to deviance, innovation or ongoing patterns of non-conformity (process), is particularly important to address when dealing with property issues. We need to go beyond oversimplification in the name of scientific method and model-generation and begin to address the empirical data in all its complexity. These and other issues will be discussed in more detail in the several chapters to follow.

THREE

From Gold to the Cross: Historical Transformations, 1591-1930

Introduction

A popular Igorot saying holds that, "Before, the lowlanders had the cross and the Igorot had the gold. Now, the Igorot have the cross, and the lowlanders have the gold." The Spanish were the first colonial influence in northern Luzon, but they cannot be solely credited with the transformation of Ibaloi society which followed their arrival. Unlike neighbouring lowlands areas, where the twin rule of the "Cross and the Crown" prevailed, the Igorots were never completely subjected. In contrast, the Americans initiated more direct changes when they entered the Cordillera 300 years later. An elder in Kabayan characterized the difference in the following way:

> The Spanish are very selfish—they do not give us anything, only deprive us, even of our food. For 400 years we are stagnant. The Americans brought us schools, even paying for the books and the paper. They gave us our present form of government. Little by little we became civilized.

Far from stagnating between the period of the first punitive Spanish raids and the first American schools, however, Ibaloi society underwent enormous change. As Scott (1974) has shown, most changes were the result of Igorot responses to new situations in adjacent lowlands areas. This chapter traces historical evidence through four centuries to show developments in Ibaloi society. As the following chapters demonstrate, some cognizance of these changes is essential to understand present-day Ibaloi society.

Ibaloi Society over Four Centuries

Gold drew the Spanish into what is now called Benguet Province; an initial expedition in 1571 was followed by more attempts to find and control Igorot gold mines. One consequence of these expeditions, and of a few short-lived Christian missions, was a few historical documents with some details about the Benguet area. The best ethno-historical sources for this region give brief glimpses of the nature of changes to property systems, social stratification and ritual life in Ibaloi culture. These sources include: for the sixteenth century (*c.* 1591), "Expeditions to the Province of Tuy" (Blair and Robertson 1973,vol. 14:281-326); for the seventeenth century (*c.* 1624), "Expeditions to the Mines of the Igorotes" by Quirante (ibid.:vol. 20:263-301); for the eighteenth century (*c.* 1755), the reports of Father Vivar on the Igorot missions (Scott 1974:116-28) and of Fray Francisco Antolin (*c.* 1788) from the upper Magat River area (ibid.:146-56); for the nineteenth century (*c.* 1830), the field records and diary of Galvey (ibid.:213-23) and the reports of the European scientists who travelled through the region a generation later (Scott 1975b). From these records, a chronology of Ibaloi property relations and social conditions from the sixteenth century to the mid-nineteenth century can be constructed.

Benguet: 1591-1624

Tuy Province neighboured on Benguet to the southeast and was involved in the pre-Spanish gold-trading network. In 1591, Spanish expeditions into this region documented the gold-producing "Ygolots" in the following way. They sometimes lived in villages of 300-400 people. They followed the political leadership and cultivated the lands of the most powerful men among them. These leaders could be identified by the numerous animal skulls on display outside their homes, the remains of ritual feasts. The people were monogamous, polytheistic, communed with their ancestors through priests called "maubunung" and dried the corpses of their dead over fires before interring them in caves. They worked copper and gold mines and some were so successful at this that they did not grow root crops, preferring to buy their needs from the lowlands. These early descriptions suggest that social stratification pre-dated the Spanish presence, although the exact nature of the relationship between the rich men and their followers cannot be determined. We do know that such reports encouraged the Spanish to send many expeditions into the Ibaloi region over the next century. The result of this harassment was a significant drop in gold production, followed by an increase in raids upon lowlands communities for slaves and cattle.

In 1624, Quirante pushed into the "Galan" mining district and there assayed ore from several abandoned works. The ore was of poor quality and this, combined with the knowledge that uplands gold miners were usually in debt to their lowlands trading partners, led Quirante to report that the fabled "Igorot mines" were overrated. He had an equally poor opinion of Igorot politics and economics, noting that they only produced a few yams and camote in shifting fields and bred dogs as their sole form of livestock. Cattle, obtained from lowlands trade, were quickly butchered and eaten in the prestige feasts of the chiefs, who were the head of their kinsfolk, one for every 10-12 households. The "sages or philosophers" were the eldest men and women, who were respected and obeyed "in an extraordinary manner." The result of Quirante's report was a generation of respite from Spanish expeditions into the Benguet region.

The contrast between the Tuy Expedition report and Quirante's report is interesting. We cannot known whether the difference is a result of changes to Ibaloi society in the intervening 33 years or a result of differing lifestyles in various regions of Benguet. Subsequent information suggests a combination of the two. Ibaloi folklore points to Quirante's period as the beginning of the gold-for-cattle trading "clans" in southwestern Benguet (Bagamaspad and Hamada-Pawid 1985, Scott 1974). These "clans" solved problems generated by the persistence of the gold trade despite the Spanish presence in the lowlands. The Spanish cut off access to the old Chinese market but at the same time introduced cattle to the lowlands; cattle subsequently replaced Chinese trade-goods in the gold trade. Acquiring cattle rapidly became a priority throughout the Cordillera; cattle-raiding soon became a menace to uplands society. Uplands gold-trading communities, with their access to cattle, were victims of such raiding, as were the lowlands towns which traded with them. Internecine violence flared along the length of the Cordillera, making travel difficult or impossible. Further, while bureaucrats in Manila were convinced that the Benguet gold mines were empty fables, local administrators in provinces neighbouring on the Cordillera continued to see gold arriving in their towns. They continued to agitate for expeditions into Benguet, using mountaineer raids on settled Christian lowlands villages as justification.

One enterprising Ibaloi named Amkidit, probably a contemporary of Quirante (*c.* 1624), was born near present-day Baguio City and married a woman from Kabayan (see Map 3). He solved both problems connected with the gold trade, Spanish avarice and uplanders' cattle-raiding by making a peace pact with Chief Mashay of Kabayan. This pact forbade, on pain of death, any residents of the Agno Valley from coming up onto the western ridge without reporting their presence to Amkidit's people. Since this ridge was the main barrier between the Agno River valley and all points west, including the main settlements on the western coast of Luzon, it was possible to monitor all travel flowing east and west over its passes. This control enabled Amkidit and his followers to reduce cattle-raiding and to limit the amount of gold going to lowlands traders. Subsequently, the valley people on the east side of the divide became dependent upon Amkidit's clan for all trade with the western coast.

Benguet: 1754-1800

By 1754, Chief Baban and his son Kidit, direct descendants of Amkidit, "belonged to a family that was steadily extending a sort of dynastic control over the western ridge of the Agno Valley from Kabayan to Acupan" (Scott 1974:117) (see Map 3). They acquired ore from other Igorots, which they refined and traded with lowlands towns. In 1754, the interests of this dynastic clan were threatened by the plans of provincial Spanish authorities. Several Ibaloi gold traders were jailed, their gold was confiscated and a punitive expedition was planned by Governor Arza of the coastal province of Pangasinan. Both Pangasinan administrators and church authorities justified this expedition by reference to the instability created by contact between the independent Igorots and the colonial population of the lowlands. In response, Amkidit's descendants sent ambassadors directly to the Governor General in Manila to plead their case. This action shows the level of sophistication achieved by the gold traders in their relations with the Spanish. In going over the heads of local provincial authorities, they gained the patronage of important government officials in the capital who were often at odds with provincial administrators. The Ibaloi were able to get the planned punitive expedition called off and their gold and traders returned (see Scott 1975a:178-82). In return, the headmen in the gold-producing region of Benguet produced the names of over 1700 potential converts in 25 towns, and agreed to the establishment of an Augustinian mission. As a result, Father Vivar came into the region and documented the changes since Quirante's time.

Mission work in Benguet was difficult for Father Vivar, since the people were highly mobile and single-minded about their business ventures. Further, his success depended on the collective agreement of the chiefs of various communities. These men consulted with each other over such issues as conversion to the new religion and Father Vivar's attempts to end slave-trading. Lack of agreement was justification for procrastinating on such decisions. Father Vivar also ran into hostility when he intervened in local practice, as when he forced his way into communities closed to outsiders during sacred ceremonies. Nevertheless, during his brief stay he noted that the towns to the west of Amkidit's trade barrier were large and prosperous, with chiefs possessing great wealth in silver currency and cattle. He could not confirm the reports of individual gold mines, since the only gold-related activity he observed was the panning done by the poor near Tonglo (see Map 3). As his mission was soon destroyed, Father Vivar had little opportunity to observe the people of the Agno valley to the east of the trade barrier.

In contrast, Fray Francisco Antolin, a Dominican father stationed on the upper Magat river to the southeast of Benguet, did get reliable information on the economic condition of the Agno River Igorots. On two occasions in 1788 he sent informants into this area (see Map 3). The first of these travelled up the valley, through Bokod and on to Kabayan, which he reported as having: "37 houses—some of them of hand-hewn boards—with ripening rice fields and herds of grazing cattle and carabaos" (Scott 1974:149). It was just before the rice harvest, and food was scarce. On the other hand, gold in the form of jewellery or bullion was abundant; the trade restriction was causing a local surplus.

Antolin's first informant could not confirm early Spanish maps which placed the oldest-known gold mines near Kabayan. He was prevented from visiting any mines or proceeding further up the valley. However, the second informant did learn about gold production, since he visited Acupan (see Map 3), one of the most productive mining districts in the valley. There he saw extensive tunnel works and was entertained by a wealthy man. He was told that the mines were handed down from father to son and that "nobody worked any mine but his own; those who had none simply panned gold in the streams" (ibid.:152). The mines at Acupan had 45 owners, who engaged in no agriculture, set their houses at the mouths of their mines to prevent theft and used slave labour in the mine shafts. Herds of carabao and cattle grazed under contract in neighbouring villages and were the miners' main source of food (or main trade item with locals) in the rainy season when contact with lowlands food suppliers was cut off.

Both of Father Antolin's informants gathered information on agriculture. By this time, wet-rice cultivation was common all along the Agno River. Cattle and slaves were trade items important to rice production; cows were payment for skilled terrace builders from northern tribal groups, and slaves were used to work the resulting rice fields. Control of labour represented wealth, and labour-intensive production innovations changed uplands culture. For example, new strains of the diseases introduced by Europeans were constantly being carried into the mountains from overcrowded and unsanitary lowlands communities. Typically Igorots responded to epidemics by abandoning infected villages, but this happened less readily in communities with rice terraces. While an epidemic in the upper Agno valley had killed so many people in 1787 that a lack of slave labour to work the rice fields resulted in widespread starvation and misery, people still lived in Kabayan and Bokod a year later.

The Benguet Igorot had developed a low opinion of lowlands living conditions. They declined the suggestion by Antolin's informant that they seek refuge in lowlands towns during hard times. They commented: "If we have gabe and camotes for food, and a little rice for our drinks, or basi, we're quite content" (Scott 1974:154). They also scorned the political organization of lowlands towns: "Among you, anybody is mayor and anybody chief, but our chieftains are always the same and no matter how much they spend, they always have some left over for other occasions'' (ibid.). It appears that political office had become a matter of ascribed status throughout the Agno valley.

To preserve their position as intermediaries between lowlands markets and uplands producers, members of trade villages maintained and controlled trails to the coast. They focussed on gold, but as Antolin's informants discovered, it was common for the elite to exact a tariff on all commercial traffic. The wealthy by this time had diversified economic interests. These included cattle-production, which required creating and maintaining pasture-lands in several different locations to prevent the spread of bovine disease, as well as the construction of rice terraces. Rice had become an important crop in the southern Cordillera by 1759; the long-delayed, punitive expedition from Pangasinan destroyed many full granaries in that year. The elite pre-ferred community exogamy since it facilitated economic diversification; affi-nal ties allowed them to establish ties in more than one community. Thus, gold-trade wealth was able to affect the economy throughout Benguet. For example, it was linked to internal usury and to resulting debt slavery.

Father Vivar abhorred the prevalence of slavery in southern Benguet (Scott 1974:123). Slaves were created in several ways: originally by raids into neighbouring ethnic regions and later by debt or punishment for a crime, as well as by birth. Mining communities had the highest demand for slaves, and the worst abuse of them, while slaves in agricultural communities were treated better. In Kabayan, slaves were imported by the wealthy to work rice fields and tend cattle; many community families trace their origins from such people. The poor, independent swiddeners were superior to slaves in social status but were often in worse economic circumstances. To improve their position, they often voluntarily allied themselves to an elite household as fieldhand or herder. Wealth implied many dependents; the wealthy house-holds comprised family, slaves, retainers and allies.

The power of any one elite in a community was said to be limited by the authority of the elders, who enforced customary law. However, it is doubtful that slaves and dependents were found sitting on such councils. True limits on power, therefore, rested in the competition between wealthy families for fol-lowers to ensure pre-eminence. I have argued elsewhere (Wiber 1989) that ritual played an integral part in the formation and control of the necessary power base, in the resulting competition between elites and in the final selec-tion of a chief or *baknang*. It was also central to the elite control of property.

Communitywide agricultural and fertility rituals were frequently men-tioned in early records. Family and individual-oriented ceremonies were doc-umented as resulting in a major drain on resources. All important economic endeavours, all life cycles and most misfortunes were marked with animal sacrifices and feasts to placate the spirits and the ancestors. In gold mining, for example, the search for, discovery and exhaustion of a vein all required the sacrifice of pigs. These sacrifices were financed by the wealthy of the community, who had the required animals. In provisioning rituals, they not only gained status but also established debts which ritual participants usually reciprocated through labour. The most elaborate rituals were reserved for the funerals of prominent people; the feasting lasted as long as the estate provided. These were rivalled in size and prominence, however, by the competitive prestige feasts of the baknang aspirants.

These rituals, along with many other aspects of Igorot culture, drew the abhorrence and thus the comment of Spanish observers. In Chapter Seven I will argue that the Spanish records of this time demonstrate the existence of three distinct types of settlements in eighteenth-century Benguet. Economic specialization, social stratification and residence patterns differed among them, while language, and certain aspects of religion and custom were probably held in common. Agricultural communities specialized in wet rice, root crops and livestock; mining communities produced gold; and the trade communities controlled the flow of gold to the lowlands and animals back into the uplands. In mining communities, residences were scattered and located at the mouths of tunnels as they were in the old-style swidden villages. In comparison, the new centres of trade and wet-rice production were tight clusters. Although the resources exploited in each type of community differed, historical records suggest the principles of ownership were comparable. Significant investments of labour in a resource resulted in more and better-defined rights. For example, the placer locations along streams were a recognized "open access resource" (Bromley 1989:205), exploited during the wet season by people from surrounding communities of all types, but mines were clearly individual property and their yield privately controlled. Social stratification was no longer based on achievement but on ascribed status. Many aspects of this eighteenth-century society are significant to the subsequent development of Ibaloi culture.

Benguet: 1800-1900

In the early nineteenth century a contraband trade in tobacco began to adversely affect Spanish colonial income from the tobacco monopoly. Ending contraband tobacco production in the uplands was the job of Lt. Galvey, whom Scott (1974:211-13) labels "the greatest despoiler of the Igorots Spain ever sent into the Cordillera." From 1829 to 1839, Galvey succeeded, mostly through the burning and destruction of Igorot communities. He led over 44 such expeditions and although he never lived to see it, Spanish garrisons were established in the Benguet region by 1848. Galvey recorded his impressions of Cordilleran life in his field journals. He visited Lutab, examined the mummy caves, wrote about the "infinite" rice fields of Kabayan and recorded the Ibaloi terms "baknan" or "petty plutocrats" and "main-gel" for those who gain prestige through military valour. His impact can be judged from later sources such as Dr. Carl Semper, who travelled through 25 years later, recording the extensive damage. In 1860, Semper saw large irrigation works, stone terraces and settlements all abandoned and blamed the Spanish for destroying an agriculture advanced beyond that of many Christian neighbours (Scott 1975b:25).

In 1848, Benguet formed a *comandancia politico-militares*, and in 1854 it was established as a province. Despite continued resistance, the latter half of the nineteenth century saw the area settled enough for several visits by German scientists. They saw a Spanish administration accomplished through the indigenous political system. For example, in 1842 the villages of the independent Benguet natives were governed by the bravest or richest men ("bacnanes"), of which there could be up to seven in each town, with the territory of the town divided among them. Beneath them were the "paupers" who cultivated the lands (Scott 1975b:6-7). By 1882, not much had changed. The province was divided into *pueblos* or townships, under a *gobernadorcillo* or petty governor, normally called *capitain*. These officials were drawn from among the local elites. Pueblos, in turn, were divided into barangays (villages), and each was under an indigenous chief known as the *cabenza de barangay*, who reported to the regional Spanish military commander. The council of elders which made up the civic authority in each village was largely drawn from elite families. The wealthy owned "the land and soil in its totality"; from them the "plebeians" must "buy their farm land" (ibid.: 125-26). Also, the wealthy owned the "iron, copper and gold mines" in which the poor had to work "at the expense and account of the Baknangs" (ibid.: 126).

In interviews with members of an elite Baguio area family in 1896, Otto Scheerer found that the eminent Ibaloi all claimed to be descended from the culture hero Amkidit, whose descendants had intermarried into each town. Nobility was achieved by keeping or increasing ancestral wealth and by observing the graded series of ritual feasts known as the *peshit*. According to Scheerer's informants, the wealthy traders were a significant driving force in Ibaloi history: promoting peace among Ibaloi villages; repressing headhunting in Benguet; and, given the development of their interests, offering little or no resistance to the organization of the region into manageable political districts under the Spanish. Their fear was that continued resistance would completely isolate them from lowlands trade connections. By the nineteenth century, they traded not only gold, but carabao and cattle, mid-latitude vegetables, coffee, tobacco and other crops. They quickly learned the profits to be had through abuse of public office under the Spanish administration. They increased their power over the poor through bureaucratic assessments. Taxation, for example, was felt most by swidden farmers. In Benguet, this tax was demanded in the form of currency (Scott 1974:291), or in "presents" of gold, cattle and produce (*Report of the Philippine Commission 1901*, vol. 3:325-29). Either way, debt peonage resulted when swidden farmers turned to the elite for loans or hire to pay such demands. This enhanced the power of the elite, who already controlled labour through debt peonage resulting from ritual.

In the late nineteenth century, the Spanish-American War resulted in American support for Philippine revolutionaries. After the Spanish were driven out in 1898, however, the Americans remained. Under their administration, certain areas, including the Cordillera Central, were designated as special zones to be administered separately by the Bureau of Non-Christian Tribes. This Bureau sent investigators into the uplands, such as Albert Jenks, who settled his wife in Ibaloi territory before working his way north to study the "head-hunting" Bontok villages (Jenks 1905, Richards 1950). Jenks found a profound difference between the Benguet natives and their "unpacified" neighbours. The Ibaloi were considered "subdued" and consequently, the least interesting of the Cordillera Igorots. Jenks argued that the Ibaloi stratified society resulted from Spanish policies of indirect bureaucratic administration. This image of the Benguet natives has remained unaltered, despite the work of Claude Moss and of later Filipino academics (Keith 1963, Leano 1958, Pungayan 1980 and Tapang 1985.)

Benguet: Post-1900

At the time of American contact, a few wealthy families (the *kadangyan*) dominated each region of the Ibaloi territory and controlled the agricultural lands and mines. The chief, or head, of the settlement was the richest, most powerful man with the widest kinship network. Only members of the kadangyan had the inherited right to compete for this position through the graded ritual cycle known as the *peshit*. Such families transferred real wealth along male lines and practised first-cousin marriage to prevent property fragmentation. They had extended households comprised of their close kin (*agi*), unpaid servants or slaves (*baga'en*), serfs or labourers under a debt peonage (*silbi*) and tenant workers who tilled the land (*aeshe*) or tended animals (*pastol*) in exchange for a share in the yield. For the *abiteg*, or common people, marriage was restricted first to members of their own class, and also to kin outside the third-cousin boundary. Despite the American ban on slavery, various mechanisms, both ritual and economic, continued elite control over the labour resources of the poor.

For example, the *encatlo* or share system between the cowherd and the herd's owner gave the herder a share of each live calf born under his care, which amounted to one quarter or "one leg." However, shares never added up to entire calves, as these could serve as the basis of his own herd. Similarly, farm labourers received no wages, instead receiving food, clothing and shelter at the kadangyan's expense. In addition, such dependents expected the ritual costs of their marriages, funerals, illness and births to be covered by their employer, which tied them in a debt of honour.

In comparison to labour, the indigenous principles of use and control of land remain controversial among historians and social scientists. It is agreed that *primi occupanis* was important, that is, the first person to cultivate land gained some definite rights to it. However, the nature of those rights and their longevity is disputed; as is the issue of how rights in different types of real estate were defined, devolved and otherwise transferred. Some argue that all land resources were treated the same under indigenous law and only at the end of the Spanish colonial period did competition over land emerge and more rigorous property rights develop (Tapang 1985). Others disagree, arguing that since field rotation was necessary to maintain fertility, the property rights in swidden fields were short term and usufruct in nature (Prill-Brett 1985). When a plot was left uncultivated for a period of time, anyone else in the community could use the land. Houselots were also held under usufruct since houses, like swidden fields, often changed location. Other types of properties, however, could be devolved or passed down to the next generation, including rice fields, houses, animals, heirloom objects, mine tunnels and slaves. There were also group rights in property which were held by the descendants of the original cultivator(s).

Ibaloi property practices were affected by new production patterns, and this has confused the picture. For example, livestock production began under the Spanish but increased significantly during the early American period with the expansion of markets for the meat. Problems with rinderpest required that animals be divided among different pastures, creating land pressures. It is unclear whether kadangyan families had to manipulate indigenous property rules to acquire pasture, since usufruct rights, once obtained, could be extended through improvements such as fencing or periodic burning. But some families had obtained land grants when a Royal Decree of 1797 made it possible to gain title from the Crown by showing continuous occupation and/or cultivation of lands for root crops or grazing. These grants were later used against competing claimants, suggesting that indigenous rules provided inadequate protection for elite entrepreneurs. Later, when American administrators wanted to redistribute such lands among the Ibaloi poor, wealthy families in each community stood by the legality of their claim to all productive lands. Such claims were supported under Section 14 of the *Civil Code* of the American administration, which allowed for the "perfection of title to public lands which had been occupied by a native or his ancestors prior to 1898; or to which conditions required by Spanish laws had been met." This issue of the nature of indigenous property rights will be discussed in more detail in the following chapters.

The effect of the American administration on stratification in Ibaloi society was to first enhance it, and to then weaken it through the introduction of education, wider employment opportunities and a more pervasive market economy. Moss (1919:237) provides an example of stratification enhancement when he discusses the imposition of American laws and the subsequent decline of the council of elders as the judiciary in Ibaloi communities. Dispute arbitration by elders was replaced by application of American law by one or two elite men (Keesing and Keesing 1934:49,110). When American law ended slavery in 1911 and curbed debt peonage by controlling the moneylenders' rates of interest, the kadangyan used their superior knowledge of American law to "land-grab." Many American administrators recognized this response but failed to prevent it (ibid.).

In time, however, with the introduction of new production, distribution and consumption patterns, stratification was eroded. Land was appropriated by vegetable farmers, native mines were claimed by American entrepreneurs, logging operations destroyed water resources and real estate values climbed dramatically in regions earmarked for development. The growing job opportunities and market in Baguio City stimulated a cash-based economy which drained labourers off the land. Mobility, both physical and socio-economic, was enhanced. In the past, surplus production was redistributed through the medium of the prestige feasts; now the kadangyan viewed public feasts as an expense rather than an investment. Upstart abiteg performed peshit, while the old elite redirected their wealth to education and the pursuit of national or regional political office. Public prestige and political power remained tied to ritual, but labour and property control through ritual debt ceased.

This brief survey of four centuries of Ibaloi circumstances has demonstrated several points. First, Ibaloi society appears to have been inegalitarian before the period of first Spanish contact, with rigid socio-economic stratification developing in the early eighteenth century. Second, the productive process underwent several changes which in turn generated several different types of communities, specializing in trade, cattle production, wet rice or swiddening. This fact affected local Ibaloi custom and practice with regard to law and property control. Finally, the privileged position of the elite declined slowly in Kabayan. Many informants vividly remembered the last days of old-style baknangs. While their families are still well-off by local standards, events in the last four decades have continued to undercut their privileged economic and political position. As the next chapter will demonstrate, current economic conditions in Kabayan are increasingly complex and precarious for all levels of society, a direct impact of the post-war period.

FOUR

The Ethnographic Quartet

Most ethnographies include the "quartet of kinship, economics, politics, and religion," which has "survived every shift of theoretical orientation, anthropological aim, and problem" (Schneider 1984:181-82). This chapter provides a perspective on the present-day Ibaloi in each of these four areas. However, it must be remembered that this quartet is artificially extracted from a larger cultural whole; divided for purposes of description and analysis, each is actually a different perspective on the same thing.

In the following description of life in Kabayan Poblacion, certain interests have determined the information provided, including property relations, social-group formation, the impact of political incorporation and economic integration, the subsequent rise of legal pluralism and of the individual strategies which employ it, and finally, the connection between the above and social stratification. These topics are interrelated; they are also very broad. Nevertheless, they provide a focus which constrains the ethnographic information of interest. For example, Ibaloi economics involves petty capitalism, market relations, distribution networks and employment opportunities not covered here (see Russell 1983, 1987). Indeed, production, distribution and consumption in the Ibaloi economy are not considered in their entirety for any one sphere of activity, whether farming, mining, small business or wage employment. The economic discussion is limited to agricultural production and some mention of mining operations. Similarly, only those aspects of kinship, politics and religion which affect rules of access to property and devolution of property rights are focussed on. In Appell's terms, this chapter delineates "social structure" as well as some features of the "opportunity structure" from the point of view of an interest in property relations. Chapter Five then shows how disputes utilize normative concepts drawn from both structures, while Chapter Six speculates on the nature of emerging structure.

Part One: Social Organization

Kinship, Social Class and Inheritance

When you round the last hill on the National Road before Kabayan Poblacion, the town appears as a small cluster of dwellings grouped along the highway. Houses all look much the same: corrugated iron roofs rusting in the sun-
shine and unpainted pine board walls. Small *ba'eng*, or house yards, are
enclosed with low stone walls, some containing a pig pen or a few chickens.
Since the houses face every which-way, there are no orderly streets or paths
between them. Some are crowded close together and others are spaced farther
apart. A few houses are visible as a scattering of dots up a ravine on the far
side of the community. The bus rumbles around another corner, past a large
school on the right and a church on the left, then past the town hall, the police
station and down and around a last hill before passing a small market. It
finally stops in front of a rather large house with a brilliant flowering tree in
the front yard and a sari sari store on the main floor. At first glance, Kabayan
appears to fill all the expectations about rural peasant villages; it looks small,
homogeneous and presents a closed face to outsiders.

After a short stay, however, the community is revealed as a cluster of
smaller units (called *sitios*), tied together by a nationally imposed, bureaucratic organization. A sense of community encompasses different boundaries
than those devised by the state. Sitios are organized around kinship, since
children often build their houses close to their parents. This residential clan-
nishness is beginning to break down under population pressure and out-
migration, but it is still discernible. More importantly, there are sharp status
and socio-economic differences between sitios as well as tensions and factions which split the community along religious, political and family lines.
Community members are not homogeneous.

In the past, socio-economic status divided the bilateral abiteg from the
elite, who tended towards a patrilateral bias, especially in the devolution of
real property. The size of a person's operative kindred remains an important
indication of economic and political prominence. However, as in other areas
of the Philippines, the kindred is not the sole basis for a following in the
"dynamics of power" (Hollnsteiner 1963, 1979). Recruitment to and relationships within ego-centred groups have much to do with social stratification. Lynch (1979:44) writes of two kinds of people in rural towns of the
Philippines: the "big," with wealth but lacking labour and political support,
and the "little," with excess labour and traditional skills, but no productive
resources. These two live in a "symbiotic union" of great stability, exchanging employment for patronage in a "vertical, personal, and revocable for
cause" relationship, stable because it meets the needs of both (ibid.:45). The
network which creates a power base is maintained through close, often emo-

tional ties of reciprocity. Such relationships depend on a continual state of *doing*, as opposed to an inalienable attribute of *being* (Schneider 1984:72). Influenced by the European-based folk wisdom that "blood is thicker than water," anthropologists often view kinship bonds as dependable, compelling and stronger than all other kinds of bonds (ibid.:165,175). This ideal state is probably nowhere applicable; in societies such as the Ibaloi, durable relationships are more often based on reciprocal exchanges of services and goods expected of one who fills a certain role, rather than on being a certain kind of kin.

Even within kinship, categorization of kin is flexible. For example, among the Ibaloi close relatives are called *agi*, more distant relatives are called *kait*. However, Scheerer (1905) documents the use of agi in reference to brothers and sisters, while I heard second or third cousins referred to as agi. Agi were once required to revenge a death or injury to ego; the larger the opposing party, the wider the agi circle was drawn (Pungayan 1980:8). If one acted like agi, then the relationship could develop into a close, effective tie. This principle of reciprocity leans on the kinship medium to form the foundation for alliances of all kinds. Reciprocity not only links people vertically through "patron-client" relationships within communities, but also horizontally throughout Ibaloi society, linking the wealthy through contract, marriage or fictive kinship (ibid.:20-21).

However, I cannot agree that such relationships are as balanced as Lynch suggests. The historic details of the reciprocal relationship between a kadangyan family and its abiteg allies suggests that the nature of the reciprocity needs to be carefully defined. In the late Spanish and early American periods, kadangyan families were known to manipulate discrepancies existing between indigenous rules of access to land, the Spanish land grant system and the American land title regulations to claim lands made productive by abiteg. Arguably, the potential for abuse is built into any patron-client relationship and was probably longstanding in Ibaloi culture; but according to their folk history, abuses became common in the late Spanish period and reached a peak during the early American administration (see also Scott 1974:288-89). During the later stages of the American administration, the situation changed once again.

A middle class emerged, consisting of downwardly mobile kadangyan or upwardly mobile abiteg (Pungayan 1980:35-36). The former were confronted with challenges to their economic superiority, attempted to reject traditional elite obligations and were met with strong resentment by other community members. Refusing to meet ritual obligations signalled a denial of kadangyan status and the obligations that went with it, including providing the poor with employment, giving material and political backing to members of the kindred, and retaining the status of the family under competition from other kadangyan families. The *mambunong* (native priest), other kadangyan, and close relatives would pressure an affluent family to "return the meat" by performing, or by funding others in the performance of, rituals. Kadangyan families who successfully resisted this pressure restricted their kindred circle and reduced the expenditures involved in maintaining status (ibid.:25). This allowed them to invest in education and new professional opportunities. Meanwhile, the abiteg were also taking advantage of new conditions. Cash-cropping with Chinese suppliers, wage employment in the new bureaucracy, or in American mining or lumbering operations, wider educational opportunities and increased marketing and exchange created opportunities for upward mobility which had not existed in Ibaloi society for perhaps a century or more.

In present-day Kabayan, the old style indices of wealth and political power no longer exist. Large herds of animals which were former indicators of wealth are gone; and people do not live in extended households with married children, tenants and slaves. Modern-day wealth is capable of wider application. Animals formerly financed ritual feasts; now cash finances these rituals as well as post-secondary-educations, emigration and consumer goods. Land, especially rice paddies, remains the single highly visible indicator of relative wealth. A family with more rice fields than can be worked with household labour is considered wealthy. People in newer, outlying sitios view themselves as "land-poor," even though many have large dryland holdings. The land-poor approach rice paddy owners with requests to *e'so*. E'so is a reciprocal term referring to a relationship between two people; the labourer provides labour, seed and water management and the crop is divided equally with the landowner after expenses are deducted. The majority of e'so cases investigated in Kabayan were between relatives.

Through such investigation of principles of access to land, a social unit was revealed which has undergone significant change in recent decades. The *bunak* is a "nonunilineal" descent group (Goodenough 1955:72). Membership consists of all individuals who can trace descent back to an apical ancestor/ancestress, whether through female or male links. The members share certain land rights established when the land was first used by the apical ancestor/ancestress. The quantity and quality of rights in such lands vary. Swidden fields, woodlots and pasture are devolved to all descendants as a group, who share equally the productive benefits. When bunak-held lands are used in the construction of rice paddies, however, the ownership pattern changes. Paddy holdings are divided and devolved in equal portions to individuals, who then enjoy exclusive use-rights in them. Such paddies are known as ancestral or inherited lands, and individual heirs hold them in trust for their children. If ancestral land is liquidated to cover culturally acceptable expenses such as funeral or curing ceremonies, the land must first be offered for sale to co-bunak members. This residual right of first option ensures that ancestral land does not fall under the control of non-kin, as this angers the ancestors, resulting in supernatural sanction.

The bunak is less important in Kabayan today; nevertheless, in circumstances of mortgage, sale or devolution, land rights are often argued on the basis of bunak connections. For example, I documented several cases of "mortgage" (*ben'ben*), with the creditor retaining use of the debtor's land until the debt was repaid.[1] In cases where the arrangement was between relatives, redeeming these lands after repayment sometimes proved difficult. Among the Bontok, similar transfers of inherited lands to fellow members of a descent-based group are not considered mortgages but "distress sales." The buyer's only kin-based obligation to the vendor is to offer the land to them at the original price, should it be resold in future. I suspect that some Ibaloi "mortgage" cases represent attempts to redefine bunak-based rights. Bontok descent-based groups remain operational in a way not possible in Ibaloi society (see Wiber and Prill-Brett 1988). This has opened the door for Ibaloi re-interpretation of the original bunak-based property rights. The decline of the bunak among the Ibaloi is discussed in following sections on property rights.

A similar confusion pertains in reference to other property-right and kinship connections. For example, recent changes to Ibaloi society have resulted in changes to inheritance. People acknowledge that state law requires equal inheritance by all offspring, but as one informant put it:

> [Inheritance] has changed because according to our custom before, at the funeral, they had to butcher pigs. If [the deceased] had a carabao, then you have to butcher carabao . . . a cow, then butcher a cow. Even if the cow of your deceased is gone, but if he had a cow before, the children must have to buy cow, or if he owned a horse, then a horse. The child who could afford to buy these animals would inherit more.

But today:

> There are some now—brothers and sisters—who quarrel about inheritance. They call some old men who voluntarily come to judge, to let them talk together until some agreement is reached. For example, we are three children inheriting. I will insist that that land was given to me by our parents. Or, if not, I will say: "That is mine because I spent more during the burial expenses." It is up to us three. Each one must have to force his decision.

---

1   Benda-Beckmann (1979:169) observed cases of this type in West Sumatra among the matrilineal Minangkabau; he termed the land involved as being in "pawn."

[Even if] there is a will—the children do not believe in it! Because one will say: "That will was dictated by the older brother because he wanted more of the land. I do not believe in that will of our father." Do you see? It is the one with the strongest will (laughter) who will inherit.

Principles of devolution seem very flexible. The formal stated rules involve pre-mortuary transfers, which at one time ensured that children could meet the mortuary expenses of their parent's funerals. These transfers normally occurred when children married and are still common.

With modern land pressures, many parents give the eldest child land to help this child and his/her spouse "get on their feet." As each successive child marries, they work this land in turn, or they may prefer an education as their inheritance. Finally, when all offspring are adults, the youngest remains with the parents, using the land to care for them until their death. This child may inherit most of the land and the original house. If the parents die while children are still minors, the land is held by an adult child or close relative who administers the property. When the children reach majority an equal division of the property should occur; however, many disputes result from administrator reluctance to relinquish control.

The formal rules, which people readily provide before going on to give examples of exceptions, indicate a continued ideal of kin-group rights in inherited land. For example, when a couple marries, they co-operate to work the land provided by each of their parents. Nevertheless, until children are born, many rights in the property are retained by the parents of the newly-weds.[2] If a divorce or a death occurs before children are born, the land of each spouse reverts back to their respective parents. If the parents are dead, the land is redistributed among the parent's heirs. Inherited lands are never given over to the spouse's family. When divorce occurs after the birth of children, the land remains with the spouse who raises them. In contrast, conjugal property is treated differently. Newlyweds are expected to open and improve new dryland gardens and rice terraces. If such improvements are not made to bunak holdings, the resulting property is not restricted by bunak member rights and may be sold or mortgaged without restriction. The couple determines how this land should be divided upon divorce or death.

There were probably always opportunities to manipulate property rules. In the past, Ibaloi communities commonly had one or more *matonton*, or older, poor individuals who were the genealogical "storehouse" of the community (Pungayan 1980:33). When disputes arose over property rights, inheritance histories or the exact relationship pertaining between two parties, the

---

2   In fact, the only rights given to the children at this time are usufruct and to the income stream (see Bromley 1989:187-90).

matonton would give evidence to a *tongtong*. This fact suggests not only that the relationship between property rights and kinship was an important one, but also that manipulation was common.

The Household

The basic unit of social, economic and ritual organization in Kabayan is the household, which is usually composed of a nuclear or stem family. Various extended family arrangements also occur, usually because of labour requirements (Pungayan 1980:28). For example, in speaking of the importance of female labour in wet-rice production, one informant commented that "Without women in the house, you must e'so your land, because if you have no women, who will do all the work?" Co-operation between households also meets labour needs, which is one reason houses are often found in family-based clusters. While households are usually small (over 80 percent of the homes are four rooms or less), membership is usually large (over 40 percent have between six and eight members).

In addition to rice and swidden land, productive resources include livestock, fruit and coffee tree stands and some woodlots. Sources of income for Kabayan households, in their order of importance, include farming, gold panning, salary, petty capitalism and rental income (see Table 1). Over 80 percent of households get some income from farming; 47 percent declared income from gold panning. Commercial income, mostly from produce sales, sari sari stores and a few farm-related service enterprises, was declared by almost 25 percent of the households. Rental income varies during the school year, but never affects more than 10 percent of the households. Almost 40 percent of the households claimed to have no regular sources of cash income, while 15 percent claimed a very small income.

TABLE 1
**Percentages of Households in
Various Income Sources**

Income Sources	Census 1*	Census 2*
Farming	74.7	71.9
Paid farm labour	11.8	10.3
Salary	30.0	39.7
Commercial	15.8	24.7
Gold panning	32.4	47.3
Rental	9.5	3.4

* The first census included 172 households,
  and the second 146 households.

The majority of households have more than one source of income, and income from one source makes possible income from other sources. For

example, earning a salary or involvement in regular gold panning often correlates with the occasional production of commercial vegetables. Patterns of
income sources also depend on the natural family cycle. Independent, young
nuclear families frequently have a single income source. Older nuclear families with adult children often pool sources of income, as do extended households. Elderly couples living alone again form single-income households.

Four levels of household socio-economic status were determined by census reports of household income and resources, particularly of land (see
Table 2). Landholdings vary widely and are the diagnostic indices of household socio-economic rank.

TABLE 2
Landholdings in Hectares
by Income Categories

	Irrigated Land	Non-irrigated Land
Lowest economic level		
Mean	.2765	.5933
Minimum	.0150	nil
Maximum	.6750	1.5000
Lower middle economic level		
Mean	.4387	1.8070
Minimum	.0486	.0500
Maximum	1.3304[3]	19.3662
Middle economic level		
Mean	.4437	2.8512
Minimum	.0500	.0700
Maximum	1.3353	16.6190
Highest economic level		
Mean	.5994	7.6930
Minimum	.0697	.7000
Maximum	1.7394	27.2500

Average income and landholdings can indicate the general standard of
living in the community, but the following discussion provides a qualitative
account of household socio-economic heterogeneity. Among the very poorest
households, landholdings are small (the mean being .2765 hectares irrigated
and .5933 hectares dryland) and usually acquired under e'so arrangements
(Wiber 1985). A young nuclear family or a single elderly person usually has
no salary or commercial income, although infrequent gold panning may sup-

---

3   As an example of the influence of rice-paddy lands in economic status, the
     household with the maximum rice-land holdings in this strata is considered less
     well off than those above it, despite holding over 19 hectares of dryland.

plement farm income. They contract their labour out when possible to meet basic food needs and express their situation by saying: "salt is our only viand" (to supplement the daily meal of rice or camote). Livestock or other productive resources are sold to meet expenses such as school fees, taxes, utility or medical bills. For many poor, basic expenses are luxuries which cannot be afforded; with little or no savings, there are few fall-back reserves in the event of crop failure or emergency. Members of these households do not occupy positions of leadership or authority. Approximately 19 percent of the households surveyed were in this situation.

The next socio-economic level is termed the lower middle-income level. Comprising larger nuclear families, with some adult offspring or extended family members, these households also have very small landholdings (the mean is .4387 hectares irrigated and 1.8070 hectares dryland). However, if a member earns a salary or pans gold, land can be rented for commercial cropping or investment in livestock. They may rear a young carabao or a few pigs, either owned outright or cared for under a share arrangement. Some households finance commercial production with credit co-operative loans. Since landholdings and the scale of production are small, the profits may only suffice to re-establish credit at the co-operative. When losses occur, the household turns to gold panning to clear delinquent debts and begins again. With the small size of the loans, delinquencies are usually a short-term problem. Some households in this category operate small businesses such as sari sari stores, swine or poultry production, bore-mills at the mining site, carpentry and other part-time trades. Members can hold positions of authority such as water distributor, barangay councillor or dispute mediator, especially if they are older men with good reputations. They will exchange labour on a reciprocal basis as well as in hire-in and contract-out labour supplies. This group comprises 38 percent of the households surveyed.

Middle economic level households have enough land to require e'so (the mean is .4437 hectares irrigated and 2.8512 hectares dryland) while they are often employed in petty capitalism. They include families with adult offspring residing at home or extended arrangements spanning three generations. They may be engaged in commercial swine or poultry production. A few professionals among the salary earners may include teachers or municipal employees. Household resources are sufficient to meet most emergency situations, but marriage of children is often delayed to prevent resource fragmentation. Commercial vegetable farming is possible without bank loans and profits are realized due to superior market and transport contacts. Some invest money in supplying other households with commercial farm inputs or in the gold trade. A few are involved in transport and vegetable marketing and may combine this with retail outlets in the community or the marketplace in Baguio City. Approximately 26 percent of the households surveyed were of this middle-income group.

A few families, comprising 17 percent of the total households surveyed, are recognized as the wealthiest households in Kabayan. Some are extended family households with members employed as professionals, within or outside the community. Some have only older members left at home while relatives reside in the larger Philippine urban centres or overseas, in North America, the Middle East or Australia. While most of these households have transferred land to children, many still retain large holdings of dryland (the mean holdings for this category are .5994 hectares irrigated and 7.6930 hectares dryland). This land is worked through e'so or rental arrangements. Included in this category are several bureaucrats or retired community officials and a household owning a number of commercial and retail outlets such as a butcher shop, general store, bar and commercial vegetable supplies firm.

All landholdings in Kabayan could be considered small, especially given that the most productive is irrigated land. Most irrigated plots are quite small in size, over 77 percent are less than 1000 square metres. Dryland holdings are generally larger, ranging in area from one-fifth of a hectare to one and a half hectares, not all of which is planted in any one season. Some dryland holdings are in the 7-15 hectare range and include holdings scattered throughout the region. This dispersed landholding pattern has led to various strategies for working the land. For example, the same household may simultaneously work a few plots held through the tax declaration program, work additional plots through e'so arrangements, hold land jointly and share the yields with related households and have one or two distant plots of their own being worked by others under e'so.

Although a high cultural value is placed on irrigated lands, which consume most of the productive energy of Kabayan farmers, households must evaluate the requirements and returns on each crop for each plot of land at their disposal. For example, dryland camote production is essential for meeting subsistence needs. Nonetheless, irrigated land can yield three to four crops per annum, in combinations of rice, subsistence and commercial vegetable crops. Rice is the preferred crop in both the wet and dry seasons; however, commercial vegetables are popular in the wet season when market conditions are favourable.

The various socio-economic levels of household do not command the same resources, nor have the same attributes, but there are important connections between them. For example, we often heard the maxim that all people in Kabayan were related to some degree or other, and these connections cut across status differences. Poor families often get help from wealthier relatives through tenancy or mortgage arrangements. Other cross-cutting ties are not based on kinship, including co-operation over irrigation activities, planting schedules and various forms of work exchange which make rice production under time constraints possible. For these, and other reasons, households in Kabayan tend to interact across socio-economic barriers more than might be expected.

Part Two: Religion

Other ties in the community are created by the factions connected to religious heterogeneity. Of the community population, 57 percent are Catholic, 30 percent are Baptist, 12 percent belong to other Protestant sects and the remaining 1 percent declare themselves pagans. But here, the syncretism of modern religious practice, in which traditional beliefs remain influential, tempers the effect of factionalism on relations between kin, the treatment of property, the productive system and dispute resolution. These traditional beliefs mix ancestor worship with a remote pantheon of gods, plus a number of spirits or *anitos* who interact more with humans (Bagamaspad and Hamada-Pawid 1985, Keith 1963, Leano 1958, Moss 1919). Those beliefs having the most influence on property involve the ancestors.

Spirits of the deceased go to dwell in a parallel world where the same socio-economic status is held as in this life. Therefore, the spirits of any animals which the dead owned during this life must accompany them into the afterworld. In the past, most of the deceased's moveable property was consumed during the funeral feasting (Tapang 1985:26). Today, funerals continue to have an effect on devolution, but it is real estate which now concerns the survivors. Ancestors maintain an interest in their descendants, especially those who manage property first developed by that ancestor (see also Conklin 1980:32). Ancestral dissatisfaction with property management can result in barrenness, madness, bad luck, poverty, ill-health and death. The mambunong or pagan priest, as they are sometimes called, intercede on behalf of the living with these ancestral spirits (*keh'daring*). Physical or mental ill-health, especially where Western medicine has been unable to effect a cure, bad luck, unusual dreams or any other deviation from the norm may result in a mambunong being summoned to trace the offended spirit and determine propitiative requirements. These usually involve animal sacrifice. Ancestors demand material objects either as redress or simply to meet their own needs in the afterlife.

Dozier (1967) compares Ibaloi, Bontok and Kalinga religions, and concludes that the Ibaloi and Bontok emphasize ancestral spirits because of their corporate, ancestor-based descent groups, while the Kalinga, who do not have such groups, emphasize nature and evil spirits. This would fit with Appell's (1976:84) argument "that the ritual symbolization of social isolates follows their entification in the jural realm." Conklin (1980:12), however, points to a similar ancestral emphasis among the Ifugao with no corresponding evidence of bilateral descent groups. Such discrepancies may relate to conditions of change, particularly in the social relations of production. The Ibaloi bunak, for example, continues to hold ritual significance despite declining importance in the jural realm. Supernatural sanctions support the residual land rights of co-bunak members, but there is a noticeable lack of corresponding legal sanctions. Inherited land is first offered to co-bunak members when acceptable reasons for sale exist. These include illness, death and sometimes marriage, all of which require ritual sacrifice. People foolish enough to flaunt this expectation became the subject of gossip in addition to flirting with supernatural danger. However, if they are "strong to withstand murmurs," there is no legal restriction preventing the extra-bunak land sale. It may also be that reluctance to proceed results more from the threat of damage to kinship support networks than from fear of the ancestors.

Other beliefs and practices from the religious realm continue to affect property concerns. The feasts known as cañao, or *mag-anito*, were not recognized as separate types of ritual by the Spanish (see Scott 1974:44) who lumped them together under one term. The Ibaloi give individual terms to such feasts, depending on the reason for performing it and the nature of the spirits and sacrifice involved. More significant events with larger attendance require more expensive and greater numbers of sacrificial animals. For example, opening a new irrigation canal or garden requires a single chicken, rice wine and the appropriate prayer. Illness may require a chicken, dog or several pigs, depending on the severity. Marriage requires several large pigs or cattle, while death may demand many pigs, cattle, horses and carabao. Moss (1919) lists over 40 different rituals practised by the Ibaloi, and most of these implicitly or explicitly affect the creation, increase or transfer of property. Death remains the single most important occasion requiring the exchange of goods between living and non-living kin. Relatives who can afford to finance the funeral sacrifices receive the largest share of land. The elders supervise this devolution of property, remember the divisions and notarize boundaries for future reference.

Property transfers associated with funerals and illness include mortgages, debts and forced sales of real estate. One informant explained:

> before, the cañao was imperative! If somebody dies and I have no pig to butcher, then among the rich who can afford it there will be one who will give the pig. Then, if the one who has to butcher has a ricefield, that will be the payment. They will do cañao. The rich man will bring pigs and get the field. Then, if the poor cannot pay [for the pig] the rich will keep the field. Yes, cañao was everything to the non-Christian. If you were sick and the mambunong told you to have a cañao, then you must have it! It might

be an "ani" or spirit who made you sick. The forefathers, the ancestors are asking, through the mambunong, for a cañao. And this sometimes still occurs. That is how the rich end up with all of it [the land].

Another man said that to know who loaned cattle for cañao in the past, one need only look at who owns land today.

Religious beliefs also retain influence in the realm of power politics in Ibaloi society. Historically, the graded series of rituals known as the peshit were the means to individual political power and as such were reserved for descendants of baknang. Today, anyone may host a large peshit-style feast and thus signal political aspirations. Candidates for municipal, provincial and/or national office often host such feasts during the campaign. The political utility of the peshit relates to the ambiguity and richness of the ritual symbolization associated with the practice.

The peshit has numerous functions: it signals political aspirations and gains; but along with several other types of cañao, it also fulfills a sacred duty towards the ancestors by honouring their achievements (Leano 1958:20-21). In Kabayan, people recognize that the cañao can redistribute wealth to other members of the community which at its widest, includes all Ibaloi. Celebrants of the peshit, for example, invite people from surrounding communities and send out animals to ensure that all share in the meat. Some interpret the cañao primarily in such an economic light; in the lack of a market economy, it allowed the wealthy to exchange excess production of consumable goods for prestige and authority (Tapang 1985:24). The mechanisms by which such generalized exchanges create alliances and social stratification are discussed by Gregory (1982) and Wiber (1989). But the cañao has a history of political functions, as well, and these functions have affected both vertical and horizontal ties. In the past, the meat-distribution requirement allowed the baknang to document the numbers of people resident in the area under his influence. Alliance ties were reinforced at the upper levels of the peshit, since kadangyan families from all the Ibaloi territory would be invited and the celebrant had to send animals to all affinal kin living elsewhere. Finally, there were types of cañao to notarize public agreements between communities and to end conflict between individuals. All of these aspects of the cañao are reflected in its rich symbolism.

And yet, some Ibaloi denigrate the cañao, arguing that it creates indebtedness and poverty in practising families. They tell of pressure to mortgage property and of families moving out of communities to avoid such pressure. A few people commented on the advantages of converting to Christianity: families are no longer impoverished by funeral requirements; those who should inherit no longer defer to those who provide the proper burial requirements; mortgages are not necessary to cure an illness or hold a wedding; and the wealthy can no longer monopolize land resources. It is true that many types of cañao are no longer celebrated in Kabayan while others have altered form. However, despite Christianity, people still enter into mortgages; they borrow money to plant a commercial crop, send their young to school or establish themselves in commercial endeavours. When they borrow, they have two options: get the money from relatives and lose the use of their land for the duration of the loan or borrow from credit institutions with the risk that they lose their land in the event of a default. There are many new drains on household income sources, and most of these have to do with political incorporation.

Part Three: Political and Jural Organization

In 1900, Kabayan was formed into a township by the Americans. Kabayan Poblacion was designated administrative capital of the township, which has survived basically unchanged. In 1909, Kabayan was combined with 13 other townships to form Benguet Province. In 1966 such townships were renamed municipalities. They and their constituent units or barangays are governed by a municipal mayor and a *Sangguniang Bayan* (municipal council) comprised of a barangay captain and several *Sangguniang Barangays* (barangay councillors). Each barangay within a municipality sends representatives to the council. These are drawn from the local barangay captains and barangay councils which manage the affairs of individual barangay within the municipality boundaries. The barangay council is composed of a representative from each sitio.

Since Kabayan Poblacion is the municipal capital, there is a resident mayor as well as the barangay captain and barangay council. The barangay captain is responsible for the resolution of all civil disputes and is the first court of appeal (after the respected elders and before the barangay court) for land disputes, divorce, rape, murder, theft and other conflicts. In most mountain communities, the barangay captain is the governing position, although the office holder is expected to work under the advice of the barangay council. In Kabayan, the mayor takes on many tasks normally performed by the barangay captain in smaller communities. As a result, the Kabayan barangay captain can assume responsibility in the organization of irrigation, although some canals rely on his help more than do others. There is also a *Lupong Tagapayapa* or Barangay Court, and finally, a community office of the INP or Integrated National Police force located in Kabayan. These bureaucrats act as intermediaries between the state political system and the local community organization. For example, the mayor is the link between the community and local and national governments. Many national and provincial administrative, infrastructure and development funds are channelled through the mayor's office. For this and other reasons, the position has the power to benefit either the entire community or only the incumbent's faction.

The power of such officials is tempered by a political characteristic common to all Cordillera communities (see Bacdayan 1976). There is a dual authority structure in Kabayan and each has a special sphere of influence. External contacts are the concern of the formalized state bureaucracy, while internal government relies on the informal leadership of the elders. Community leadership, whether in economic, political, social or religious matters, is enhanced by kinship and economic ties. Those with wider networks are more influential in local affairs. Such respected elders (the females are called *aba'kol* and the males are called *na'ama*), can be called upon to aid individuals who are in conflict or in emotional difficulties. Their greatest skill is effective listening. In the formal dispute resolution forum or tong tong, they attempt to guide the disputants to reconciliation. They rarely dictate, but rely instead on commonsense and good conscience to prevail. However, they also have the leverage of their social networks and a set of well-known and respected normative concepts concerning property relations, family law and civil torte.

The tong tong has many characteristics considered common to indigenous, or non-Western, dispute-resolution institutions (see, for example, Benda-Beckmann 1979, Hayden 1987, Kladze 1983). Each case stands alone and without reference to precedent. Outcomes are not predictable, as the desired result is one on which all parties can agree, the "amicable settlement." Mediators do not so much rule on a case as manage the dialogue through which an outcome is negotiated (see Hayden 1987). Evidence suggests, however, that here again Western observers have oversimplified things. For example, in Kabayan's past, disputes were resolved in an autocratic fashion when conflict developed between people who were not social equals. We were told of cases where corporal punishment was meted out for an offence against a social superior; these offences ranged from "bad talk" to theft and debt default. In a few extreme cases during the early American period, the transgressor was hung by the heels until dead. Moss (1919) also documents arbitrary methods of establishing guilt, including trial by ordeal.

These examples of judicial rulings and corporal punishment are very different from present-day practice, which resembles more the conciliation panels required by state law in the administration of justice through village courts. At tong tong sessions which I attended, the only way elders could keep people talking was the suggestion that recalcitrant disputants take their case to the state courts. The state legal code's approach to property and family law is often unpalatable to local people; this reminder is enough to keep people involved in highly frustrating and prolonged discussions. This tong

tong process and the "amicable settlement" it strives to reach are touted as the customary ancestral way, despite all historical evidence to the contrary.

Community gossip indicates that dispute cases in Kabayan run the gamut of types discussed by Comaroff and Roberts (1981:231) in their model of dispute. The more intractable cases, as is consistent with that model, occur where individuals "in the cause of their competing constructions of reality" (ibid.:236) strategically appropriate and manipulate normative conceptions. The situation is only made more complex when a condition of normative pluralism prevails. Then the process of dispute resolution can provide opportunities not only for the combatants but for the competing authority structures as well. The elders of Kabayan have created a customary past which legitimates their present role in dispute resolution, a role essentially designed to offer an alternative to state authority. So multiple normative orders increase the opportunity for strategic manipulation of norms by combatants, and local distaste for state courts and codes generates opportunities for the development of local alternatives. The resulting legal pluralism creates opportunities for further complexities in conflict over dispute-resolution venues.

Disputes in Kabayan often escalate through several levels of venue. Disputants usually begin with conciliation by older relatives, sometimes move on to a formal tong tong, then on to the barangay captain, and finally on to the village court. Few cases reach the national court system; most problems are resolved at the community level. Intercommunity conflicts have also been resolved by meetings between the parties in question and their village courts.

These courts are a recent innovation, established in 1978 by presidential decree. There are between 10 and 20 members who are drawn from the ranks of the elders, appointed by the barangay captain and subject to the peoples' approval. Conciliation panels consisting of three members are drawn from this larger membership and these can be selected by the disputants. Cases are heard at the request of the barangay captain or the police. The majority of cases taken to the municipal or higher courts must first be heard by a village court.[4] In the few decisions I read, rulings were based on a mixture of commonsense, customary law and the state legal code. This syncretic characteristic of rulings in local property disputes can be estimated from the cases discussed in the following chapters. But in order to understand the strategies of normative appropriation and manipulation employed in these cases, it is first useful to examine the "rule book" of the Kabayan property system.

---

4   The court is excluded from cases involving the government, offences not involving a private party, or offences punishable by more than 30 days in jail or fines in excess of 200 pesos (although this last clause is sometimes ignored).

Property Rights

Tracing connections between people and property in present-day Kabayan is an exercise in frustration. Property falls into several categories in terms of its type and the rights held in relation to it. This is true in any property system. But when one utilizes the descriptive meaning of legal pluralism as discussed in Chapter Two, the inherent complexity of any property system emerges and must be considered. For example, despite state government attempts to promote private property among Cordilleran people, rights in most resources are rarely viewed as individual property. In this section, patterns of access to land, water and gold will be discussed to demonstrate this fact.

Many resources in Kabayan today *are* individually managed and some are devolved directly from one person to another. But land is often held jointly, as with conjugal property or land inherited collectively by siblings. The community forest reserve is labelled a communal resource, as are water and gold occasionally; however, the local understanding of what communal means must be carefully qualified. The Kabayan Credit Co-operative operates under state co-operative regulations. One can solicit rules about rights in property and then compare them to actual patterns of management, use, benefit or transfer. When these comparisons are done over a long period of time, it becomes obvious that the above patterns are influenced by factors such as the existence of and the discrepancy between external and indigenous normative concepts and the consequences of the interaction of the two. Kabayan has had 200 years of external contact, and it is difficult to unravel the introduced from the indigenous and to provide a record of how these have been appropriated in individual strategies. Historic data provide clues to current disputes and property-relation problems in Kabayan, but I save discussion of these diachronic developments for later, focussing here on the current situation of stated rules and observed practice.

Land

In the initial census of 182 households in Kabayan, 141 (77 percent) declared access to land, while the rest declared themselves to be landless. Those with land usually justified their rights by reference to "ancestral" title. In the Cordillera, this refers to two concepts: the general tribal or community-based rights to resources, or more specific rights devolved to descendants of ancestors/ancestresses. However, few people in Kabayan can rely exclusively on either of these meanings to generate rights in land. To understand how people do make claims to land, it is necessary to discuss both state and indigenous views on tenure.

In many Cordillera communities, local control of property relations is intact (Conklin 1980, Drucker 1977 and Prill-Brett 1985). A cyclical pattern of property ownership is common, with various types of rights generated by the nature and extent of productive improvements made to the land. Land within community territorial boundaries is open for economic exploitation by members. Tenure in land is generated by either individuals or groups through labour inputs. Improvements of a long-standing nature create most of the rights Bromley (1989:187-90) lists as common in liberal ownership, including possession, use, management, benefits, security (perpetuity), transmissibility, and execution to settle debts. The right of capital benefits (alienation, consumption, destruction), however, are subject to restrictions based on rights lodged at the community level (alienation, appropriation) and in kin and non-kin based groups (alienation, devolution). Such lands include rice paddies, burial sites, orchards and managed woodlots.

A more restricted ownership is generated by short-term improvements; rights are limited to possession over a limited term, as are use, management, benefits and transmissibility. Examples include pasture and swidden plots in which rights may have devolved to the descendants as a group. Where community endogamy prevails, over time any one descent group will include most members of the community. At this point the land will once again be treated as an open resource. There are variations on this cyclical pattern (Aranal-Sereno and Libarios 1983, Conklin 1980, Prill-Brett 1985) but for most uplands people, the Ibaloi among them, the basic outline is consistent.

In contrast, the Philippine state has a different approach to property; I will demonstrate that this has served as an "opportunity structure" for individual Ibaloi. The state recognizes two types of land: public and private. Public lands are under the management of government agencies, such as the Bureau of Forestry. In private lands, the liberal range of rights are granted to an individual in return for taxes which are paid proportionate to the land's economic productivity and value. The tax-classification scheme designates seven economic categories of land: wet rice, camotal, vegetable, fruit, pasture, virgin and residential lands. The arbitrary nature of this scheme is apparent in Kabayan, where fruit trees are planted on residential lots or within camotal fields, virgin land (as well as much of the land classified as "public" by the government) is usually land not presently in use for swidden or pasture, and vegetables are often planted in rice paddies. In Kabayan, the main distinction is between wetlands or *payew,* of which there are approximately 34 hectares listed in the tax records, and drylands or *uma,* at close to 152 hectares.

Tax registration requires the approval of the local tax assessor, who visits and confirms the size, location and productivity of the field. This is not always possible due to terrain, and the limited resources of the tax office, so lands are not always accurately registered. Once a plot is tax registered, the state grants rights in the land, but these are limited. For example, the owner must pay taxes, but the state denies any protection from appropriation and limits security of tenure in other ways. If taxes are paid for 10 years without default, private ownership may be granted. However, in Kabayan, the government suspended title-processing after passing legislation to protect the watershed of the Ambuklao hydroelectric facilities. All lands within this watershed (including most of Kabayan Municipality) are designated public. Aranal-Sereno and Libarios (1983) discuss the conflicting nature of legislation affecting tenure in the Cordillera Central. Nevertheless, in recent years, most of the land within walking distance of the community has been registered through the tax-declaration program.

A second problem is that private titles that do exist are out of date. Inheritance divisions, mortgages, sales and other property transfers within the boundaries of one title have not been officially documented. One reason relates to the lack of cadastral surveys in the Cordillera, which makes legal description of a parcel of land difficult and expensive to acquire. Consequently, the same parcel often falls under more than one tax declaration. Alternatively, landholders have sometimes listed the property of several individuals under one declaration. Family lands may be registered under one name long after subsequent divisions because of the expense involved in transferring titles or tax declarations from one name to another. In the case of small parcels of land, a group of siblings often agree to list it under one name while sharing the proceeds among them. Many years may pass without trouble, but land disputes in such situations are common.

Adding to these problems are government regulations affecting upland tenure which have recently multiplied and which are often contradictory. None of these fully recognizes indigenous practice (Lynch 1983, and Prill-Brett 1985). For example, the Revised Forestry Code, Section 15 (Presidential Decree 705) designates all land over 18 degrees of slope as public and under the management of the Bureau of Forest Development. This ruling would affect most Ibaloi landholders, since most land in Benguet Province lies at more than 18 degrees slope, but where such lands are cleared and in agricultural production, the law has not been strictly enforced. In fact, in 1974, Presidential Decree 410 gave "ancestral landowners" a grace period of 10 years to secure title for their lands. When this regulation expired, most Cordillera landholders had failed to meet the deadline. Few could afford the costly process to register land, and with conflicting state regulations, many were frustrated in the attempt to do so. For example, the Revised Forestry Code states that where trees are still standing, there can be no private tenure (Lynch 1983:20-21). And so farmers "accidentally" burn trees off land and declare it for tax registration, while Bureau workers plant seedlings to extend their sway over swidden sites. Presidential Decree 1559 (1978) allows for the forcible removal of minority landholders at the discretion of the government. This facilitates grants of land to private enterprise or government agencies for resources extraction. Displaced landowners are relocated to government "resettlement" areas, but past relocations have been a disaster for participants (Aranal-Sereno and Libarios 1983:451).

In the second household census completed at the end of the fieldwork period, household heads were again asked the number and size of plots worked by their household and how rights to them were established. The data resulting from better-informed questions is suggestive of future problems for this community. Just under 60 percent of the plots were held by individuals under tax-declaration certificates; joint or family tenancy accounted for 19 percent; 6 percent were held under mortgage; and lease or e'so accounted for 15 percent, although people estimated e'so as representing as much as 30 percent of land held. Significantly, 21 percent of the plots worked by community members are located outside the community. The figures suggest the difficulties faced by future generations. For example, the length of time that present owners have held their land indicates the growing scarcity of suitable virgin land for agricultural expansion: 42 percent of the plots have been held by their present owner for 25 years or more; a further 22 percent have been held for between 10 and 25 years; 16 percent for between 5 and 10 years and 20 percent for less than 5 years. The small size of holdings also indicates that further fragmentation is impossible. Only a high rate of out-migration to Nueva Viscaya, Baguio City and other regions has eased the situation in the last generation. Ironically, as uplanders have migrated out, lowlanders have left their overcrowded homes in increasing numbers to press into the uplands. This fact has increased uplanders' desire to secure government recognition of their tenure in land.

Water

As with land, both state and local tenure regulations have influence on access to water in Kabayan. In the traditional allocation of water rights, as in land tenure, the most important principle is *primi occupanis*. The first person(s) to develop a water source and to build irrigation canals and rice terraces establishes rights in that water, including use, management, and transmissibility. However, the Ibaloi view possession (Bromley 1989:187-90) as a problematic right when applied to water. As one elder said: "You cannot control the water because, after all, water flows!" Excess water draining from the tail end of an irrigation system is therefore a free resource. However, when further paddies are constructed using such water, their owners have fewer rights in the water. During a dry year, such tail-end paddies cannot demand a share of the water as can the original members of the irrigation system. This relates to the historic pattern of irrigation development in Kabayan.

When these systems were constructed, the builders contributed to costs in proportion to the amount of land they intended to irrigate. Subsequent distribution of the water was proportionate to paddy size; each of the original paddies had connected to it the right to enough water to work it. The present-day owners of these paddies are entitled to that water. Glick (1970) calls such tenure "the Syrian model" to distinguish it from a contrasting system where land and water are kept distinct (Yemenite) and in which each can be sold separately. Water in the "Yemenite model" is distributed through a fixed-time measurement of water "shares," which can be sold like any other form of property. This does not occur in the "Syrian" type of system. The fact that irrigated land and irrigation water are inseparably linked has certain implications. In Kabayan, a farmer has the right to draw irrigation water from a canal that serves his/her land, although recently the following restrictions have applied: the share cannot be drawn if the land lies unproductive; it cannot be channelled away to another field, nor sold to another party. At the beginning of each planting season, farmers within a system make their plans and needs known at a general meeting. The water is subsequently distributed according to availability and the amount of land and crops to be planted. Farmers in the system co-operate to protect the sources of irrigation water from encroachment. However, tail-end paddy developers are not part of the system and only have rights to water in times of excess.

In her book on management of "common pool resources," Elinor Ostrom (1990:30-31) develops terms useful for distinguishing the types of people involved in irrigation in Kabayan. She speaks of: *resource systems* (such as irrigation canals) as yielding *resource units* which individuals appropriate or use "without harming the stock or the resource system itself" (ibid.). There are three categories of persons or groups involved: *appropriators* or those who withdraw resource units; *providers* or those who arrange for the provision of the system and *producers* or those who actually construct, repair or take action to ensure that the resource system yields units. The original constructors of a system were providers, producers and appropriators. In the present day, heirs of the original constructors are producers and appropriators, while tail-end field constructors (as well as tenants of field owners) are appropriators who may or may not be producers. Ideally, however, all appropriators should contribute to production costs with maintenance labour.

Challenges to these arrangements, however, have developed in Kabayan history, and since the state has a slightly different view on water rights, "opportunity structures" have been utilized in those disputes. Prior to the

1935 Constitution, the government view was based on the Spanish *Law of Waters* (1866) which had similarities to Ibaloi practice: "surface waters which fall or collect upon an estate belong to the owner while flowing over the said estate" (quoted in Cruz, Cornista and Dayan 1987:25). This made private control of water possible. In the 1935 Constitution, natural resources were designated state property; however, the state continued to recognize private tenure in resources such as water. This changed in 1976, when a new *Water Code* expressly repealed private tenure in water. Water rights are now an administrative concession through a water permit which is obtained from the National Water Resources Council. Application must meet numerous requirements, including evidence of ownership of the land to be irrigated, a location plan indicating the point of diversion, the co-ordinates of the site determined from a professional survey, clearance from the Provincial Irrigation Engineer and the Public Works District Engineer's Office to determine that the proposed use will not interfere with any present or future projects or plans for local water supplies, and a hydraulic engineering determination of the litre-per-second requirements of the proposed use for the water. Without a state water permit, no ownership can exist relative to water.

Although people in Kabayan were informed that under the 1976 regulations they have no legal right to their water, several things ameliorate any concern about the situation. First, according to the explanation of the new code offered to local people, individuals or groups with private tenure in water under the old water regulations have first priority in gaining the new permits. As long as no one else applies for rights in their water, many people in Kabayan feel that their use of the water is protected. Competing claimants for water use, such as industry or commercial mining, are unlikely to emerge. No one in Kabayan that we met was planning to protect their access to water through application for a water permit. However, this was not always true. The various water-related disputes to be discussed in Chapter Five demonstrate the problematic relationship between land rights and water rights in Kabayan.

Part Four: Economic Production

Livestock

At one time Kabayan was one of several Benguet livestock-production centres for swine, carabao, cattle and horses. Herds were primarily owned by the kadangyan, but even the poor had a few pigs and chickens for ceremonial occasions. The number of grazing animals forced farmers to fence dryland fields, and stone walls can still be seen around old garden sites. Today there is little need for fencing. Livestock production in Kabayan has sharply declined in the post-war years as it has in Benguet Province in general (see Tapang

1985 and Lewis 1992:124-26). Reduced numbers of the native species of pig are still raised in Kabayan, but the larger imported pigs favoured for commercial production require expensive feeds, making their cost prohibitive for most producers. Cattle are very rare; only one household has a viable herd. A few goats and chickens are raised, but most of the fresh meat and eggs sold in sari sari stores is imported from the lowlands. Meat is not considered a staple for most families.

Today, horses are a luxury. The only draft animal employed in the village is the water buffalo. It is essential for plowing, harrowing and levelling the rice paddies and is the centre of many complicated loan and tenancy arrangements. Buffalo are expensive by local standards; an immature male or female can cost 3000 pesos, a large adult male between 5000-6000. There is a long period of care and expense before animals become an economic asset, since they cannot be worked until they are between five and seven years old. Buffalo are expensive to maintain because of the difficulty in acquiring forage. Former open-access pasture areas have been tax registered by a few individuals who now charge fees of 10 pesos per month for grazing. Many owners prefer to cut grass from mountainsides and carry it down to their stock, but the more practical solution for households without spare labour is to pasture on the lands of a relative or friend in other communities. This practice is still called *pas'tol*, after the traditional caretaking agreement (Tapang 1985: 11-12). The caretaker of the animal is responsible for providing fodder, salt and general care. In return, the caretaker receives a share, called *bi'ngay*, of all offspring born to the animal, as well as access to the animal's labour.

Buffalo are usually privately owned, but their expense and caretaking arrangements affect access and use. In Kabayan, 39 people own buffalo, holding a total of 59 grown animals and five calves. During the land-preparation season, these people rent their animals for a fee ranging from 50-250 pesos. The fee is on a contract basis per area of land and depends on the owner's estimate of the time required to do the work. Often people are unable to pay cash, and then other arrangements are common. For example, the person borrowing the animal may prepare the owner's land in return for the use of the animal on his own land. Often animals are loaned to relatives by both owner and caretaker. Buffalo are an asset not only as draft animals but also as the means to gain access to land. Landowners who want a sharecropper to work their land look for someone with access to a buffalo. Since production costs are deducted before the rice yield is divided, landowners try to keep costs such as draft-animal rental fees to a minimum.

Cropping Patterns

In Kabayan, the most important productive resource is land. Land uses include wild forests for building materials and fuel; woodlots for products such as avocado, coffee, rattan; grasslands for grazing and runo (canegrass) supplies as well as for dryland garden fallow. Sunny, protected slopes close to settled areas are valued for dryland gardens, while rice terraces are constructed in areas where permanent water sources and terrain allow. Human intervention has resulted in a vertical ecology landscape (Brush 1977), with forests on the high mountainsides, woodlots, gardens and grasslands on the mid-range slopes and terraces in valley and ravine.

Several major cropping periods overlap to create a continuous annual round of activities. Two crops of rice are produced annually: the irrigated dry-season crop composed of native varieties known as *kintoman*, and the wet-season, rain-fed varieties called *talon*. December to February is taken up with preparations for the dry-season crop: irrigation canals are cleaned of several months accumulation of weeds and washed-in soil; seedbeds are prepared, and you see the men and their water buffalos preparing land with several rounds of soaking, plowing and harrowing. The women uproot, bundle and prune the seedlings when they are eight or nine inches tall, before transplanting them. They also weed the rice paddies twice before harvest and clean the walls surrounding the rice paddies of all vegetation so that the ripening grain is not shaded. Just before harvest the fields abound with bird-scaring devices and small children to drive pests away. Harvesting is done by hand with a small curved blade. The rice stalks are fed to livestock or beaten into the paddy mud as mulch. Harvested rice panicles are grouped into bundles called *bu'tek*, which are about six inches in circumference, holding close to five kilos of husked grain. They are the unit in which yield and field size are discussed, the common form for grain storage and a sort of currency in Ibaloi society as the basis for traditional rates of pay.

Wet-season rice production begins in May or June. Because of the rigours of the wet season, talon plants are often sterile, but even these less certain returns are vital to subsistence.[5] The importance of the wet-season crop can

---

5 We heard conflicting reports on the origins of talon rice varieties. Most people agreed that talon varieties originated in the lowlands but differed on the dates of introduction into Kabayan. A few argued that except for a variety called "California," which was introduced during post-war famine relief, talon varieties are indigenous to the uplands. However, kintoman varieties are generally tall, photoperiodic and require up to eight months to mature. Most talon varieties are dwarf, ripen in three to five months and are not photoperiodic. This argues for an origin in the high-yield varieties of the Green Revolution.

be determined by the problems it causes for the primary dry-season crop. The introduction of talon changed the kintoman schedule. Kintoman was originally planted in December, growing and ripening in the ideal conditions of the dry season. Yields were higher then and the plants more resistant to disease and pests. For this reason, the old people disapprove of planting talon, saying that it "eats" the kintoman.

In addition to rice, most households plant dryland gardens (*uma*) on the steep hillsides. Towards the end of the dry season men burn off the ground cover, uproot the larger, tougher shrubs and grasses and leave the women to turn, loosen and cultivate the soil. Planting commences with the first rains, and crops include the traditional camote and increasingly commercial vegetables such as corn, peanuts, peas, beans, tomatoes and onions. Soil fertility rapidly depletes in dryland gardens, and while camote does well for several years before a fallow is required, commercial vegetables demand chemical inputs. Compost, green manure and long fallow are rarely employed since the introduction of commercial fertilizers, pesticides and herbicides. For this reason, it is expensive to plant commercial gardens, and alternate sources of income affect the amount of vegetables grown.

Factors affecting production levels in dryland gardens are cultural as well as economic. Despite the fact that camote yields are high (Lizarondo, de la Cruz and Valdellon 1979), people in riverine settlements such as Kabayan devalue it as a food and argue that it is too much work. Vegetable gardening, on the other hand, offers an opportunity for cash income if it can be financed. As a result, the average market price of gold affects not only the numbers of people involved in gold panning or mining, but also in commercial gardening. When gold commands a good price, many young people pan gold until the beginning of the wet season, when they use their proceeds to finance commercial gardens.

Vegetables are increasingly planted in selected rice paddies as well. Reasons include water shortages, surrounding peaks shadowing the paddies and higher altitude causing cool night temperatures, all of which harm rice but do not prevent commercial cropping. However, market gardening fluctuates in Kabayan. When market prices for vegetables are very good, even the best rice fields may be planted to vegetable crops. On the other hand, when prices are low people will return to planting rice and camote, as well as arboreal cultivar such as banana, avocado, coffee, mango, sugarcane, pomelo, areca palm, jackfruit and pineapple. Bananas, mangos and coffee are the most common of these cultivar; all are used for home consumption as well as for sale. This mixed production system places unusual demands on household labour supplies.

Labour Sources

In Kabayan, a clear but flexible sexual division of labour is apparent. In rice production, men build and repair terrace walls and irrigation systems, manage water, prepare fields, clean rice stalks from harvested fields and prepare seedbeds. Women soak seeds, plant seedbeds, transplant, weed, harvest, dry the palay, store, pound and cook the rice. Either sex will clear vegetation from paddy walls, turn water into fields, chase birds away and bring palay in from the fields. In uma production, men burn, clear, and break the soil in the field and apply chemicals. Women cultivate the soil, plant, weed and harvest crops. Men tend to manage commercial crop production, especially making arrangements for purchase of cash inputs, transportation and marketing. Satisfying the number and timing of these labour requirements strains the resources of every household. In an economic census of 42 households along one irrigation canal, a total of 22 054 hours of labour was declared by all household heads for the last crop cycle, whether applied to rice, sweet potato, commercial production or some combination of the three.[6] This works out to an average of 538 hours of labour per crop cycle for each household.[7] In the census, 13 815 hours (or 63 percent of the total for all households) were provided by household members. Three other forms of labour arrangement make up the balance. Table 3 provides information on labour arrangements, their relative application to three crops and the percentages of each labour type employed in producing each crop.

Several factors influence labour recruitment from outside the household, including the development cycle of the nuclear family, the number, sex, health and ages of family members, and specific tasks to be performed. Some tasks are labour intensive and must be completed in a short time, including rice transplanting, weeding and harvesting. Other tasks such as plowing, harrowing and levelling the paddies require specialized tools, skills or a draft animal which the household may not have. The arrangements made depend on the task, ready capital, kinship ties and existing mutual obligations. In general, there are three labour arrangements common in Kabayan: *o'buan, a'tang* and *pol'deya*.

In contrast with commercial agriculture communities, people in Kabayan still practise o'buan or the traditional, reciprocal exchange of labour, although

---

6 This figure was calculated on the assumption of an eight-hour working day. Farmers claimed this as the norm, considering the need to rest during the hottest hours of the day, the constraints of daylight and of other household task requirements.

7 Remember that each household may participate in up to four cropping cycles per year in combinations of rice, camote and vegetables.

it occurs in some sitios more than others. Historically it was common in jobs which could not be handled alone and which were shared by all community households at one time or another, such as building a house, a stone wall or a rice paddy. Today, these are normally performed by cash labourers, but other situations still call for o'buan. Examples include a group of friends aiding each other in repetitive tasks such as weeding, cultivating uma soil, harvesting rice or camote and *kom'boy* or backpacking produce out from isolated fields. A group of workers completes the task and is fed a meal by the recipient household, who then owes each member of the work party a reciprocal amount of labour on a similar task. O'boan may also be used to overcome a temporary problem such as a family being called away and needing others to tend their fields.

TABLE 3
Household Expenditures in Agricultural Labour by Labour Type and by Crop in Person/Hours and in Percentages*

Labour type	Rice		Vegetables		Camote		Total	
	Person/ Hours	%	Person/ Hours	%	Person/ Hours	%	Person/ Hours	%
Household	6 120	47.3	3 205	75.4	4 490	92.6	13 815	62.6
Pol'deya	2 298	17.8	1 048	24.6	360	7.4	3 706	16.8
A'tang	3 141	24.2	0	0	0	0	3 141	14.3
O'boan	1 392	10.7	0	0	0	0	1 392	6.3
Total	12 951		4 253		4 850		22 054	

* That is, the percentage of the total requirement for labour for that crop provided by that labour type.

A'tang is another traditional form of labour recruitment. People contract their labour to landowners during rice transplanting and harvest. The same workers who transplant usually return to harvest, and receive a bu'tek of palay per day of labour. If they only come for either transplanting or harvest, but not both, labourers receive one half bu'tek per day. A'tang is still popular in Kabayan for two reasons: first, it ensures a labour supply during the crucial peak labour periods; and second, it gives landless or land-poor families access to highly valued, traditional varieties of rice.

In market gardening, producers prefer pol'deya, which is paying field labourers a daily cash wage. Many gardeners do not have surplus rice to pay workers, since they plant the more profitable vegetables in paddies they lease or own. Daily wage rates were 15 pesos for a male and 12 pesos for a female in 1983. This rate is similar to that paid a'tang workers; the medium of exchange is different but the evaluation of labour is similar. The government had set the market price of rice in the three to four peso per kilo range, despite the many devaluations of the peso during this period. Consequently, the daily salary for male pol'deya workers was roughly equivalent to five kilos of rice per day.

Since people now require cash for utility bills, taxes, school costs and agricultural inputs, pol'deya agreements are becoming more popular among the labourers. On the other hand, a specific type of labour remains popular among employers for certain agricultural tasks. For example, o'boan is common for rice-paddy weeding; a'tang is associated with transplanting and harvest; pol'deya is connected to labour-intensive tasks where a high degree of drudgery and a low degree of skill are required, with the exception of plowing and harrowing. Approximately 25 percent of the households hired labour for tasks involving draft animals. In rice production, household labour supplies over 47 percent of the required labour, followed in order of preference by a'tang, pol'deya and finally o'boan (see Table 3). In subsistence vegetable production, household workers perform over 90 percent of the labour, while pol'deya workers make up the balance. In commercial vegetable production, household workers perform 75 percent and pol'deya workers the remainder of the required labour.

The household prefers to exert some control over those tasks which most affect yield. Therefore, pol'deya labour is rare during harvest (only one household hired rice-harvest labour) and is not used for seed planting and chemical application. Seed, fertilizers and pesticides are expensive inputs in commercial farming, while poor harvesting practices represent one of the largest areas of post-production loss. Workers who are paid a daily cash rate are not as careful during harvest as one who gains a share of the harvested crop. Employers prefer a'tang workers for rice harvesting.

In a mixed cropping system, farmers require flexibility. Labour patterns are just one area in which Kabayan farmers have attempted to maintain a degree of choice in their production decisions. Variability in cropping decisions is also reflected in the census figures: 90 percent of the 42 households planted rice during the surveyed crop cycle, 61 percent planted camote and 34 percent planted commercial vegetable crops, indicating that most practise mixed production. Households need a flexible pool of labour to satisfy their complex labour needs. In addition, those households with more labour than land find that the present system allows them to intensify labour and increase productivity without obtaining more land. This is a boon in the typical peasant situation of land shortage and growing population base. However, land is not the only scarce resource in Kabayan.

Irrigation

Irrigation was described to us as the "life blood" of Kabayan by local officials. Rice terraces follow the contours of the ridges and valleys wherever sufficient water is found to irrigate paddies (see Conklin 1980:15-16 for a discussion of terrace construction techniques). These water sources all originate on the upper slopes of Mount Ambobongan and Mount Al-Al, which lie to the northeast of Poblacion and rise to 2248 and 2318 metres above sea level respectively. The drainage from their slopes forms two creeks which empty into the Agno River below Poblacion (see Map 5). Water intake for irrigation systems occurs where perennial springs are found along these creekbeds; sites where water wells up with sufficient force to be tapped as the headwater for a canal system are called *talek'bed*. Sources of water in the community are limited, overtaxed and threatened by watershed deterioration. Every year some tail-end paddies are not planted due to water shortages, and even domestic supplies are threatened. Schemes to improve the situation are often under consideration, but alternative sources are far away or already committed, funding is limited and water remains scarce.

Irrigation in Kabayan is based on technologically simple gravity systems, comprising diversion weirs, shallow ditches or *kola'kol*,[8] and flumes (called *tar'oy*) which carry water over gullies and fields to individual paddies. The systems are largely constructed of local materials such as stone, bamboo and pine logs, flattened tin cans and rope, although imported cement, plastic hose, metal pipes, steel cables and preformed cement culverts are occasionally seen. The level of engineering skill demonstrated in the design of systems is impressive. In some locations, canals have been bored through solid rock, and in others, extensive rock riprapping has been used to line canals where discharge rates vary widely in the rainy season. The highest intake point is found at 1700 metres above sea level and the descent from intake to final paddy in the overall terrace structure is accomplished in approximately two kilometres of steep terrain. Canals often stretch over several kilometres of rough terrain before reaching the target terraces.

---

8   This term means "to dig" or "to scratch" according to Fray Antolin, who heard it in the late eighteenth century in reference to Nabaloi gold mining (Scott 1974:149). Scheerer notes that it means, among other things, an irrigation canal, a hole bored through something or an awl (1905:153). Scheerer (1905:143) also documents the following Ibaloi irrigation-related terms: *sibog, man'ibog* and *mam'pa'sibog* for "irrigation," "to be the one who irrigates" and "the one who will be ordering the irrigation," respectively. These terms suggest an interesting division of interests and labour; however, they are not commonly heard in Kabayan today.

The physical characteristics of the irrigation infrastructure suggest one large communal system. However, I argue that Kabayan has 13 independent canals and 34 hectares of rice land which is divided into corresponding terrace sections to form small, named irrigation systems. In addition, there are several small, individually owned terraced areas irrigated from small springs. Each of the 13 independent canals is subdivided by branch canals which irrigate field sections sharing the same name (see Maps 6 and 7). Within field sections, there are further divisions based on feeder canal service areas. Feeder canals, branch canals and major canals each represent a level of organization in the irrigation groups that manage irrigation in Kabayan.

These groups are loosely structured and there is no formal irrigation society in the community, despite government organizational efforts. There are no membership lists, fees, charters, official leadership or authority hierarchies as are common in the lowlands (Lewis 1971). The relative virtues or flaws of a highly flexible, democratic, segmented and informal social organization are rarely discussed in Kabayan, although town officials did describe this as the "customary ancestral" form of "communal irrigation." But there is little agreement on the real nature of the "communal" groups. For example, there are two broad trends of thought regarding the basis of membership in irrigation groups, corresponding to the two sets of people normally using irrigation water.

Most farmers hold that the current owners of the *original* rice paddies are the only legitimate members of an irrigation group because they all have inherited rights to water from that irrigation system. According to this view, people who subsequently opened rice paddies using excess water draining away from the system are not members of the irrigation group. In contrast, others claim that water is a communal resource, the benefits of which all are entitled to share. This group holds that if a person works land irrigated by an irrigation system, and contributes labour co-operatively to maintain the infrastructure, then that person is a member of the group with a right to sufficient water to make their land productive. The nature of this disagreement will be addressed more fully in Chapters Five and Six. Here I will convey some idea of the complexity of land and water access, and of irrigation organization by reference to a single Kabayan irrigation system.

Taxation records for the land within one irrigation system were cross-checked with kinship charts and census forms. The 12 hectares of land was registered to 60 individual owners. Of these, 12 individuals (or 20 percent of the total), are deceased and their land is administered by a relative. Each of the 60 landholders are or were members of one of six major families or four minor families. Major families are defined by representation in community genealogies for at least three preceding generations and by a kadangyan background. Minor families are defined by their recent appearance in genealogies; most acquired land within the preceding generation and identify themselves as offspring of slaves or *sabo* (outsiders). These major and minor families have affinal interconnections; in fact, when all affinal linkages are traced, no single family is isolated. Clearly, marriage barriers between kadangyan and abiteg had broken down; genealogies indicated this happening in the period surrounding World War II. The census records showed another 26 families gaining income from the land through tenancy or land rental. Thus, in this one irrigation system, 86 households made some income from the 12 hectares of irrigated land.

The nature of this one system suggested some things about resource use in Kabayan and about changes to the property system. For example, fractionalization of holdings and increased population pressure on irrigated land has reached a serious level as a result of the breakdown of traditional methods to control both. The present-day degree of relatedness between households in this sample suggests that kinship plays a significant role in access to increasingly scarce resources. Participation (as opposed to membership) in an irrigation system has increased as rights in land and thus water can be acquired in several ways: inheritance, purchase, sharecropping or lease. People who work the land are responsible for all aspects of production, including water application, and thus become participants in canal meetings and work groups. Farm families send a representative from their household for each co-operative labour day announced by canal leaders, whether for repairs, maintenance or cleaning. Most farmers work plots scattered among several systems and must send a representative to each, a fact which has encouraged irrigation systems to stagger days of labour. All who benefit from a system share equally in meeting labour needs, but in other respects, not everyone is equal.

Traditional leadership and authority within irrigation systems demonstrates this fact. In Kabayan leadership is situational. Leaders are chosen from among community members who are respected for their personality, economic standing, family background and knowledge of local custom. They fill roles in the community which are often informal, without title and without national bureaucratic sanction. Irrigation leaders are usually influential community members who own more rice land or lands covering a larger proportion of the field section along any one canal. When the farmers along this canal gather to discuss irrigation, such individuals are deferred to and become *de facto* leaders. Decisions are reached through consensus, but often consensus depends on the charismatic qualities of acknowledged leaders and their seniority in kinship and landlord/tenant relationships.

In interviews with 42 household heads along one canal, people were asked to identify their canal leaders and often went on to identify field-section leaders as well. These people were described as "active elders" with "wider rice fields." They motivate the group through their personal industry and organization; for example, by being the first to dry plow, they indicate that the time has come to clean the canals. They ask the barangay captain to serve formal notice of upcoming meetings and then inform him of majority decisions so that these can be enforced. They are the first workers on canal maintenance or repair days. They reproach shirkers and those who steal water, break agreements or do not co-operate in general. Their ultimate threat as they verbally upbraid such individuals is to deny them water, although people stressed that it has never been necessary to do this. These leaders are also valuable in dispute settlement because of their knowledge of traditional divisions of water between field sections and of the history of the development of the system.

During the dry season, most Kabayan systems follow a water-rotation practice which results in intermittent flow to the paddies. The distribution schedules are arranged to make maximum use of the water without individual paddies experiencing water stress. At the beginning of each dry season, water-rotation schedules are arrived at by common agreement of the farmers involved. At the same meeting, farmers will decide on hiring a water distributor (*man'dapis*, or "the one to be distributing the water"). The man'dapis may be elected from among those volunteering, or the original paddy owners may appoint someone. All responsibility for water delivery up to and including individual paddies rests with the man'dapis unless farmers in a field section agree among themselves to turn the water into their own fields. As the responsibilities end when the rains begin, the job lasts for only a few months. The salary is based on a per-paddy assessment of palay, averaging four bundles per field. The position is very demanding for two reasons: first, most canals operate on a 24-hour rotation schedule; and second, farmers are often dissatisfied with the water received, the behaviour of neighbouring field-owners or with water delivery decisions and tend to direct anger towards the man'dapis. The position may not be filled every year; it depends on the volume of water in the creeks and streams and the timing and amount of rainfall received at the start of the wet season.

Although canals are independent, sometimes they are forced to co-operate. Water sources are often so close together that depleting one causes levels in the other to drop. Landslide damage can threaten water supplies for several canals. During dry-season land preparation, water demands peak when available water supplies are at their lowest. When the available water is only sufficient to soak paddies in one field section at a time, intercanal agreement allows the upstream canal on the water source, and the upstream field section on this canal, to monopolize all the water for land preparation. Water continues to flow from springs downstream, and if this is sufficient, other field sections will also begin land preparation. However, locking the available water up in paddies to create the muddy conditions necessary for land preparation usually reduces the downstream flow until the majority of irrigation intakes are affected. Once upstream field sections and/or canals have completed land preparation, the bulk of the water is then channelled into the next field section or canal and so on, down the drainage system, until all canals along the stream have had their turn.

Co-operation within irrigation systems and also between systems was good during our stay. However, serious irrigation disputes have occurred in the past (see Chapter Five), and there is the potential for them again in the future. Serious conflict is related to difficulties experienced in adjusting to social, political and economic change. For example, some tensions were apparent over water-allocation problems created by vegetable plots. Kabayan has remained the cultural heartland of the Ibaloi, but as with other Benguet communities, outside forces have a continual impact. Kabayan farmers continue to plant rice and camote, but in recent years, cash-cropping has increased.

Commercial Gardening

Since World War II, market gardening has become a flourishing agribusiness in this region of the Cordillera. Halsema Highway, which travels north from Baguio City into Bontok Province, was the earliest artery connecting mountain people to urban centres and markets in Benguet Province and beyond. This road has encouraged many mountain people and immigrants from lowland areas to open commercial gardens, thus transforming the countryside around it. Vegetable production also expanded into nearby towns. The impact of this agribusiness is felt in different ways in different communities. As one example, the production decisions and marketing strategies in Kabayan diverge sharply from other communities, such as the neighbouring town of Loo Valley.[9]

Commercial vegetable farming was stimulated by dealers from Manila and Baguio City who were mainly ethnic Chinese. These entrepreneurs came to the Philippines with cash-cropping expertise and capital for investment, but after 1934 they were denied land ownership under the national policy of the Philippine Commonwealth Government (Jensen 1975:34). Under several arrangements these dealers continued to promote vegetable production in

---

9 I am grateful to the Cordillera Studies Center (CSC) and especially the Loo Valley Research Team for the information which made this contrast possible. See also Lewis (1992) for a contrast with Buguias.

mountain communities. Sometimes they became silent partners in a farm, providing the capital and expertise for a local landowner. Sometimes they became "suppliers"; this term has come to mean any person who provides the capital and market connections for commercial production. Seed, chemicals and cash for hiring labourers are provided to the farmer and the resulting crop is sold to the supplier at a price fixed by them.

During the early years, the number of producers was low, while crop prices were high. Uplands farmers prospered, as did their suppliers. Soon, however, vegetable production spread to other areas of the Philippines. The rising price of petrochemicals drove the cost of inputs up at the same time that market crop prices fell. Caught in their obligations to their suppliers, uplands farmers fell into debt, despite opening new lands and expanding their production levels. Smaller operators (with farms less than half a hectare in size) were disadvantaged in regard to capital sources, technological application and labourers; as a result, the yields of these farms were generally lower and losses were more consistent. However, even larger operators were experiencing losses (Lizarondo, de la Cruz and Valdellon 1979:32).

Several factors prevented a return to subsistence farming, including environmental factors which made newly established communities unsuited to traditional crops, and increasing population pressure. Another significant factor was the nature of financing commercial gardening. Most Cordillera farmers prefer not to borrow from formal credit institutions, which charge them interest and require clear land ownership for collateral. In contrast, interest charged by suppliers is a hidden one taken in the form of lower farmgate prices, and suppliers do not demand collateral. Suppliers also provide services, including delivering inputs to the farmgate, making marketing arrangements and arranging for crop harvest. But under worsening market conditions in the early 1980s, this relationship between suppliers and farmers deteriorated. Farmers sold crops to the highest bidder despite previous obligations to a supplier, claiming typhoon or pest damage. Suppliers tightened their co-operation with each other, setting vegetable prices among themselves and threatening to take delinquent loans to court. When farmers tried to break their debt peonage by approaching government-established rural banks for production financing, they discovered they had no market for their crop due to supplier monopoly on retail outlets. Further, one bad season meant a foreclosure by the bank, and the rules governing formal credit agencies usually operate to the benefit of larger landholders. As a result, many farmers continue to rely on suppliers for operating capital (Jensen 1975:140; see also Davis 1973 and Russell 1987).

Credit problems are not the only factor which contribute to the worsening situation of vegetable farmers in areas of the Cordillera. Farmers cited the following as major problems for upland commercial vegetable producers: insecurity of land tenure, insufficient capital and credit arrangements, marketing difficulties, transportation problems, scarcity and high cost of farm inputs and information on their proper use (including seed, fertilizers, pesticides),[10] and finally, lack of reliable irrigation. Marketing problems include dependency on middlemen for market information, the fluctuation of market prices, lack of post-harvest technology such as packaging, grading and proper transportation of produce to market, inadequate bulking and debulking centres and the lack of co-operation among producers.

Kabayan farmers struggle with all of these same problems; however, the commercial farming experience has been different in Kabayan. Environmental, historical and social factors have contributed to this difference. Kabayan is located in an environment suited to traditional crops. While farmers had experimented with commercial vegetables from the late 1800s, suppliers developed an interest in the community relatively late. Until the National Road was built in the late 1950s, any commercial crop had to be back-packed over an intervening mountain range to a pre-arranged pickup point on the Halsema Highway. While the scale of production increased in the 1960s, chemical fertilizers, pesticides, seed supplies and equipment demanded cash which was not readily available. When suppliers approached the community, Kabayan farmers borrowed from them. However, prices offered by suppliers were never comparable to reported market prices, and as input costs climbed, Kabayan farmers began to fall into debt.

Farmer response to this situation was a small, co-operative movement to resist supplier price-setting, and this in turn prompted a local businessman to establish a co-operative savings and lending institute in Kabayan. This credit co-operative opened in 1972 and now has 1000 members with combined financial assets of close to 2 000 000 pesos. The impact on vegetable production in Kabayan has been interesting, particularly for small-scale farmers with intermittent involvement in cash-cropping. The majority of such farmers borrow production capital from the credit co-operative. Loans are extended in amounts up to twice the member's savings account balance. The loan committee will respond to an application within a week, in comparison with rural banks, which take months to process a loan. Most accounts are between 500 and 1000 pesos, so the average loan is around 2000 pesos. In the case of a few large depositors, loans of up to 30 000 pesos have been made, although

---

10 The CSC researchers found that vegetable farmers in the Loo Valley often concoct potent brews of many different kinds of pesticides and herbicides and apply them to a crop every 6 to 10 days during the growing season, whether or not there are signs of pest or disease.

the policy is to restrict loans to 10 000 pesos or less. Loans may be in the form of cash, or a combination of cash and farm inputs from the co-operative seed and chemical supply store, which has organizational and technical assistance from the Ministry of Agriculture.

The Kabayan Credit Co-operative (K.C.C.) is organized along guidelines provided by the National Bureau of Co-operative Development. It is a member of the Co-operative Union of the Philippines, of the Ilocos Region Co-operative Union and of the Provincial Federation of Co-operatives. Its only branch is in Poblacion, but other communities within the municipality have been assisted in organizing their own co-operatives, and their funds are held by the K.C.C. under a trust fund agreement. Further, local organizations such as the Parents'-Teachers' Association deposit their funds in the K.C.C. The co-operative follows banking policies established by the Development Bank of the Philippines, which sets rates of interest and other banking policies. Anyone may open a savings account in the K.C.C., and this has provided vegetable farmers and other business entrepreneurs with a source of capital. Further, the co-operative is the institutional linkage for several national agrarian credit programs so that money is available for establishing small businesses. These national credit programs have often experienced a very high default rate, but this is not the case in Kabayan, according to the K.C.C. secretary. The local vulcanizing shop owner, for example, managed to clear the original debt and expand his operations through a second loan. Some vegetable producers became delinquent on their loans but always managed to finally pay their debts. Financial institutions of this nature are rare in Cordillera communities.

Borrowing from the co-operative offers several advantages over the alternatives. Farmers do not lose the use of their lands as they do with mortgages to relatives or friends. They can sell their crops to the highest bidder, usually to the regular vegetable dealer but sometimes to a *poesto* (market stall) owner or bulk dealer in Baguio City. Jeepnie drivers are frequently commissioned to take a load of vegetables to Baguio City on a per kilo arrangement. This means that farmers can eliminate at least one middleman and obtain a better price. They felt it was better to scale down operations and borrow when possible from the co-operative, thus avoiding debts to suppliers.

One advantage Kabayan farmers have is the fact that their community is the municipal administrative and business centre. Since it contains municipal offices, schools, market, hotel, shops, rice mill, a vegetable dealer, several full-time jeepnie drivers and a daily bus service to Baguio City, the commercial activity and opportunities for employment mean more cash is available. Farmers can borrow from employed relatives or friends, and the usual agreement is a 50-50 split after expenses are deducted. A similar arrangement may be made with a poesto owner in the Baguio City Market who provides a regular outlet for the crop and the necessary capital for production in return for regular supplies of fresh produce. One final important source of capital in Kabayan is *sayo*, or gold mining, as well as *pan'se'jew*, or gold panning.

Local mines are very small scale, but when luck is with the miners, sacks of *nava* or gold-bearing soil may generate an important cash income. This income may be erratic, but a surprising number of families are dependent upon *sayo* for all or part of their subsistence. During the school vacation period, membership in the miners' association rises to 300 or more. Parents complain that teenagers leave school once they become involved and that the money is spent on alcohol and "travelling around." Others argue that mining provides employment for the underemployed and the initial capital for vegetable production, commercial enterprises, and in some cases, higher education. Families involved in cash farming have at least one member involved in gold mining. A jeepnie driver in the community obtained the down payment for his vehicle from an unusually productive sack of nava.[11] Drawbacks to mining include the hard and dangerous work involved for miners, a lack of water for washing the gold and landslides that are sometimes caused by the tunnelling.

Taken together, these opportunities to acquire capital for vegetable production from sources other than the vegetable dealers and/or the banks have meant that producers in Kabayan have been able to avoid the heavy debt load that has plagued other uplands farmers. Kabayan farmers can also maintain subsistence farming alongside commercial production, or revert to it when market prices are too low or input costs too high. Following the assassination of Benigno Aquino in 1983, the Philippine peso was devalued several times, making the cost of foreign imports skyrocket. Farmers in Kabayan reacted by scaling down or eliminating vegetable production. Input costs were lowered by reducing the amounts of chemical inputs and growing vegetables for which the seed could be cheaply obtained. These strategies are possible, first, because Kabayan fields are generally suitable for rice production, and second, because farmer debts are small, can be allowed to fall delinquent for a time and because farmers are not being pressured by suppliers. As a result, farmers in Kabayan are in a better position to withstand setbacks in the commercial vegetable industry.

The importance of flexible production arrangements cannot be overstressed. Davydd Greenwood (1976:142-43) wrote: "I think flexibility should

---

11 In contrast, another regular jeepnie driver borrows his vehicle from a lowland compadrazgo (see Dart 1977:19) with whom he has to share his proceeds. Others work as drivers and are paid a salary by the vehicle owners.

be considered [traditional agriculture's] defining characteristic, as contrasted with the specialized, market-oriented and market dependent form which has emerged with the spread of agricultural capitalism.'' The failure to recognize this flexibility as vital to the survival of farmers can be disastrous. Agricultural capitalism does not always provide a reasonable rate of return or a secure lifestyle (see Durrenberger 1984:6-7). In fact, Western agriculture, the role model for agricultural development planning in most less developed countries, is facing a crisis of increasing proportions. Recently, the post-war policy of promoting high input/high output models of farm-system management has been increasingly criticized, and ironically, some analysts are suggesting that we look to the flexible traditional farm management system in order to learn more about viable lower-input, labour-intensive regimes (see Raymond 1985).

Conclusions

This chapter has drawn data from each aspect of the traditional quartet, politics, religion, economics and social organization, to both provide background material for succeeding chapters and to establish the important connections between property control, kinship, political incorporation and economic integration. Having established the historic and present-day productive patterns, we can now proceed to examine the patterns of dispute in the community over the past century.

FIVE

Property Dispute: A Study of Consequences in Legal Pluralism

Property systems have three component parts according to Appell (1974:4): "(1) a scarce good or service; and (2) the constellation of jural interests, along with their supporting sanctions, with respect to this scarce good that are held by (3) a social entity." Scarce goods and services in Kabayan society were discussed in the previous chapter, as were some aspects of the accompanying jural interests. These jural interests and their supporting sanctions will be explored more fully in this chapter through an analysis of property dispute, before going on in the next chapter to address the third component, the social entities concerned with property in Kabayan.

Identifying social entities concerned with property is a problem because of conflicts occurring at two loci: within and between structures (as generated by competing jural systems and their attendant property concepts) and as a result of process (especially the competitive behaviour of knowledgeable agents). In terms of property structure, Appell (1974) notes that there are various formal organizational options. A social entity concerned with property may be a single individual or a group of individuals. When more than one individual is involved, rights in property may be divided among them in two basic ways. Rights may be held in severalty as when each member holds property rights as an individual, but there is a bond creating a group in the fact that such rights are held by a number of people in the same piece of property. On the other hand, property rights may be held by members of the group "as if they were one." Further, all of these formal types of property-holding groups may or may not be recognized in the jural system. Appell finds the distinction between groups recognized in the jural realm and those not so recognized to be an important one. The "jural entities" are "legitimate" emic categories; recognition in the legal realm becomes the test of methodological validity. However, if competing jural systems define these social entities and their property rights quite differently, how are we to decide which entities are legitimate?

Legitimacy may not be the best focus in property-system research. If we instead turn our attention to how law motivates individual, goal-oriented behaviour we may gain a better understanding of the "social significance" of law (see F. von Benda-Beckmann 1983, 1989 and Vanderlinden 1989). Further, we will be closer to understanding how individual goal-oriented behaviour affects law (see Wiber 1990b). Law and the interpretation of laws, like behaviour, is always changing; in what way can the former be an indication of the emic reification of the latter? Nowhere is this more problematic than in property law. In this chapter, I examine several cases of property dispute to demonstrate the utility of the concept of legal pluralism to an understanding of the social significance of law. In Kabayan, such dispute has had consequences for property-holding entities and the rights they have. These cases are tabulated in Table 4.

TABLE 4
Subjects of 29 Cases of Dispute
Resolution in Kabayan

Land	11
Water	8
Gold	5
Civil/Family	5
Total	29

People raised the majority of these 29 cases of dispute in the context of my discussions with them about property. Two were documented while attending tong tong sessions, and two more were taken from village court records. Many of the same "notorious" cases were recounted by a number of different people and the accounts sometimes varied, particularly in chronology. Some disputes date back to the last century; a few cases probably occurred between 1912 and 1930, and the majority took place in the period after World War II. Of the most oft-heard cases, 11 involve land, 8 involve water (irrigation) and 4 involve gold; the rest include civil cases and family disputes. Some cases have overlapping subjects. The information gathered on these cases is hearsay, based on memory and folk history; it is therefore subject to all the possible errors of such sources. Nonetheless, when we are interested in law in the *social field*, hearsay allows us to grasp the grass roots *perceptions* of law and to see the effects of that perception on behaviour.

Land Disputes

A common pattern prevailed in the 11 cases of land dispute; socio-economic stratification played an important role. In the past, an individual consolidated land through several processes: inheritance, improvement of bunak land or of community land, and finally, mortuary and other forms of "distress mortgage." Land then served as the basis for political power by attracting retainers of several types. Control over labour allowed for the improvement and consolidation of yet more land. As allies and dependents grew, so too did political influence. In the period following the establishment of the American administration, another strategy was added to the above repertoire. Wealthy individuals often had the political knowledge and wherewithal to register lands under state law, whether traditional rules gave them exclusive possession of the land or not. As the Kabayan tax assessor put it: "Well, if you are in the position to know something and other people do not then you take advantage. So maybe you submit the requirements and get title even if someone else owns it." It is common to hear claims that state title was acquired despite the fact that others had rights in portions of the land under indigenous practice. When the lands were registered, these people were forced to become tenants on their own land. Traditional prestige reinforced by state bureaucratic power prevented resistance during the titleholders' lifetime. Once they died, however, these holdings frequently became the subject of disputes. Tax assessors sometimes contributed to the problem by granting tax registration to the so-called tenants. Their motivations are said to include ignorance of local conditions and/or sympathy for the plight of the tenants.

In Kabayan, for example, stories are told of the last "old-time baknang," an individual called Kamista.[1] It is said that due to his affluence and his position in national politics under the American administration, Kamista obtained state title to numerous tracts of land in Benguet Province. The Kabayan tax assessor showed me three such titles, issued in Kamista's name in 1912, covering an area presently cultivated by several unrelated households. These families now dispute Kamista's right to the land and Kamista's title has not prevented them from farming the land or from registering it under the tax-declaration legislation. It is the opinion of many local people that state title granted during the American administration was often gained under false

---

1 Kamista's name has been changed in this account, as have all Ibaloi names, to ensure anonymity. A few of these people were immortalized in Moss's publication on Ibaloi songs, one of which contained reference to selling items to the man I call Kamista (Moss and Kroeber 1919:188). Other elite in Kabayan's folk history are also mentioned there (ibid.:190). These are the characters in local gossip and folk stories about village disputes.

pretence. Applicants claimed their land on the basis of "ancestral" rights of cultivation or pasturage, but in doing so misrepresented indigenous rules, since these did not grant exclusive rights in most kinds of property.

On the other hand, descendants of title holders represent history differently. They often refer to a notorious case involving a kadangyan's coffee plantation. In 1915, a slave belonging to the kadangyan was appointed to guide a government official who came to Kabayan to survey and title lands. When the titles were issued, the coffee plantation was found to be in the name of the slave; meanwhile, the slave disappeared and sold the land to a third party. This case is said to still be "in the courts." People who recount this tale do so to argue that the elite class created economic opportunities in their communities and were repaid with duplicity by people who had less right to the land than they. To complicate things further, in a similar tale Kamista sold a former slave some land in the full knowledge that this man would then develop rice terraces by stealing water from a neighbouring canal owned by Kamista's political rival. Although the slave later sold the land and moved away, he left behind an irrigation conflict which continues to this day. Many stories of this kind are attached to Kamista's estate, suggesting conflicting interpretations of past historical events.

Numerous disputes over the Kamista estate are said to be tied up in the state court system, a venue selected by one or more of the disputants since the cases involve state tenure regulations. When some elders were asked how they would rule if these cases were adjudicated in a traditional tong tong, many supported Kamista's opponents. Their view was that abuses occurred during the American administration because indigenous practice was imperfectly understood by state bureaucrats. Elite families intermarried and their members had rights in the same bunak lands. Development of pasture or swidden did not create exclusive rights in the land; even paddy development left residual rights among co-bunak members. Land-grabbing by an elite using state title was often at the expense of other wealthy families with equal or superior rights in the land. Some stories refer to cases where paddy lands improved by one bunak member were then appropriated by a relative through state title, although these stories are normally peopled by social unequals. Only one of the 11 cases of land dispute documented in Kabayan did not involve state title. In this case, the two heirs of a kadangyan could not agree on a division of the land. A stalemate developed which the elders had not yet resolved.

Five other land disputes documented in Kabayan involve the infamous block titles which were granted in the Cordillera during the American administration. Block titles covered several holdings, but title was granted under the name of one individual. Sample cases concern a significant area of rice terraces below Kabayan Central, as well as the site on which the municipal buildings were built. Here there is greater consensus in the stories; heirs of the title holder are said to be squeezing out other legitimate but undocumented property owners. The elders of the community have solved some cases by informing the tax assessor's office of the history of the land and of the rights to it, with subsequent tax registration granted to those supported by their testimony. The tax assessor pointed to the increasing number of cases involving such titles being heard in courts all over the Cordillera, most of which involve defaults on bank mortgages. Competing claimants to the land are brought to the bank's attention when it attempts to foreclose.

In one case, a parcel of land containing several houselots was titled in the name of an individual since deceased but survived by one daughter. This woman acquired a bank loan using the title to establish collateral. Meanwhile, each of the individuals with houselots on the land acquired tax declarations. When the woman defaulted on her loan, the Kabayan tax assessor had the unhappy task of determining what land to take to cover the debt. As most title descriptions of land in this region rely on a 1909 survey, based on markers since removed or relocated by local people, accurate legal descriptions of land are rare. He was aware that other tax declarations could show up with boundaries that overlapped the titled property. He advised the bank to survey and foreclose on four hectares which did not interfere with other tax-declared lands. In other cases, landowners were forced to pay more than their land was worth to clear a debt they did not incur. Problems created by block titles are well known in the region and have become ammunition in family battles. For example, one young man created a crisis in his extended family by threatening to sell land held under a block title to finance his immigration to Hawaii.

All 11 land disputes have proven difficult to resolve for many reasons, not the least of which is the differing interpretations of past events. Modern-day politics is also playing a role. In the uplands, for example, tribal land claims are being used to dispute state designations of land as "public." In support of these claims, Cordillera politicians and civil rights lawyers argue that Igorot communities practised communal land tenure since "time immemorial." Historical documentation suggests otherwise, as will be demonstrated in Chapter Seven, but political expediency always influences understanding of history. If this "communal" strategy were successful, state title issued to indigenes on the basis of local concepts of individual ownership could be considered as invalid as the designation of other lands as "public." The local management of communal holdings would be a contentious issue, and individual property rights of possession and management would be affected. As I will demonstrate, the communal argument has already affected gold and water resources.

The success of an argument for cultural uniqueness based on a communal background can be gauged by President Aquino's 1987 decision to include the Cordillera in the regions granted semi-autonomy under the revised constitution of the Philippines. This decision would have had significant impact on the uplands property system had the subsequent referendum accepted the proposed *Organic Act* to govern such a Cordillera Autonomous Region. However, in early 1990 the population of the Cordillera voted for a resounding rejection of the semi-autonomy package in all but one of the five affected provinces (see Wiber and Prill-Brett 1991). As a consequence, the issue of legitimate rights to land, and of the balance between group (including state) rights versus those granted to the individual continues to be debated. This debate has affected competition over many productive resources, as I will demonstrate first with irrigation disputes, and then with gold disputes.

Water Disputes

Among the people of Kabayan, there is one conflict which is universally credited with bringing about changing local perceptions of water rights. The case again involved Kamista and developed as a consequence of a short-lived, commercial mining boom during the American administration. According to local accounts, an American prospector alerted Kamista to the commercial prospects in a local gold deposit site. Kamista responded by first obtaining state tenure to the site on the basis of ancestral grazing rights and then by staking a mineral claim.[2] This occurred sometime before 1936, which supports Fry's (1983:179) claim that the gold rush of 1930-35 resulted in challenges to indigenous land- and water-use patterns. Foreign prospectors and mining companies, as well as many local elite, ignored indigenous property rights during this rush (see also Tapang 1985:30-31). Kamista dug a canal to supply water to his mine site for ore processing and began tunnelling with the help of American mining engineers from the Baguio gold fields. This alarmed landowners in Kabayan, since piping water to the mine site threatened supplies to the downstream rice paddies. So far as local people were able to determine, Kamista's mine operation proceeded legally under the freehold system of American law, where "a prospector who staked a valid claim only needed to perform two hundred pesos worth of assessment work annually in order to maintain his property rights" (Tapang 1985:30). Consequently, the elders could not enforce indigenous rules of priorities for

---

2   There is some disagreement in the accounts as to whether or not Kamista actually obtained a state mineral claim, but people agree that the rumoured existence of this claim, together with Kamista's social standing, was sufficient to prevent challenges to his mining activities during his lifetime.

water use. As a result, another prominent landowner within Kabayan named Dukat decided to seek state protection for his water needs.

Dukat persuaded the landowners along two irrigation systems to contribute funds for obtaining water rights, one for each source. Dukat has since died, as have most of the people involved in these applications. However, one male who participated became a key informant for my study. He claims that the two titles were obtained and that the documents listed the name of each beneficiary and protected their water rights "in perpetuity."[3] Since the mine shortly proved unviable as a commercial operation, it was never necessary to challenge Kamista in court. Dukat left the title documents with his son when he died. This son claimed to remember the documents but could (or would) not produce them, so I attempted to track them down by visiting several government offices in La Trinidad and Baguio. An official in the Public Works Department denied that water rights were pursued by mountain people in the past. He commented that "Igorots" were only now beginning to protect their water sources as a result of National Irrigation Authority funding policy; if communal systems want financial development assistance they must meet certain guidelines, including gaining state rights in the water. He categorically denied that any title was issued to Kabayan irrigators in the past. However, many people in the community claim to remember the documents well since they were used in several water disputes which developed after World War II.

The failure of Kamista's mine did not put an end to problems that gold mining created for irrigation. In the post-war years, members of the community made small tunnels at the site and began using the old mine canal to bring water for ore processing. The downstream irrigators forced miners to restrict their water use to the rainy season by threatening court action, using the state water title. This agreement was respected for two reasons. First, many of the miners also owned or worked rice terraces in Kabayan, and second, this small-scale mining was not based on any state-recognized mineral rights. The miners were not willing to take the issue of water rights to court. However, mining continues to result in disputes. One man told me of a dispute in which he, as representative for the miners, was held responsible for a major landslide and was taken before the provincial authorities. He was released because, in his words: "Fiscal _____ was given something to drink and became friends with the miners and he forgot everything and dismissed the case." The old mine canal remains central to disputes between farmers

---

3 Some claim that this title protected water access from December to May only, others that it had no limitations.

and miners, since Kamista sold it to an in-marrying male who has maintained and extended it to develop terraces below the mine site. So far, public pressure has kept the new owner, and the miners, from diverting water into the old mine canal during the dry season. But this situation is precarious because mining is too dangerous during the wet season.

The next major irrigation dispute in Kabayan resulted from government attempts to boost post-war agricultural production and thus tax revenues. In the early 1950s, the government encouraged agricultural expansion with legislation opening public lands to anyone willing to farm it. According to the man who was tax assessor in Kabayan at that time, local officials were to facilitate this process. People who could not normally afford state title were soon acquiring land under the tax-certification scheme. After 10 years, these certificates were convertible into individual title if no pre-existing claim was documented. Acceptable substantiation of competing claims to land included title from either the Spanish, American or pre-war Philippine governments.

This legislation soon created problems for people who claimed to have acquired title before the war. During the war years, there was a tremendous destruction of public buildings and a corresponding loss of public documents. Some elders claim that many of the so-called public lands that were tax-declared were actually lands owned by families under previous state title. But their ownership was difficult to prove because of the wartime destruction. The situation was also bad for people whose rights to land was based on local practice, which the government had never acknowledged. For example, in Kabayan, the "public" land most often selected for development under the new legislation lay in wasteland areas along canals between the headwater of an irrigation system and the rice fields supplied by that system. The strategy was to acquire land with a potential for irrigation development. Because of the value placed on rice paddies, new fields were soon put into rice production, using water taken from the pre-existing irrigation systems. Historically, opening gardens along pre-existing canals was forbidden, as the new fields would lay between the irrigation source and the original fields, making it difficult to regulate appropriation. However, the new state tenure regulations prevented the original landowners, those providers, producers and appropriators in Ostrom's (1990:30) terms, from fighting encroachment on the system.

The original landowners appealed to community elders to resolve this situation. In tong tong meetings, the elders suggested that people opening new paddies only appropriate water from pre-existing canals during the rainy season. However, after a few years this agreement collapsed; water theft, crop and field sabotage and even violence became common. Many people told of sleeping in their fields at night to protect their crops during this period. Only the landowners within the two irrigation systems which had obtained state water title during the mining dispute were in a position to threaten court action to protect their water rights. Along these two canals, therefore, a situation developed in which *both* sides employed state law to support their rights; the new appropriators took water to irrigate land held under state legislation, while the original providers and appropriators supported their claim to the water with state title. One might assume, therefore, that the state was able to resolve their conflict. However, in my research I documented eight cases of irrigation conflict, three of which were resolved within the tong tong setting. For the rest, arbitration proceeded to state adjudication venues, with none of the resulting judgments solving the problem.

The reason for this failure rate lies within an interesting aspect of the interaction between state and local jural concepts. In one case, irrigation system producers and providers brought new appropriators to the municipal court. It is said that they cited their water title as evidence in the case. The court is said to have ruled that the *priority* in water use belonged to the older rice fields but that new landowners also have a right to water. The court further suggested that the same principle applied to tail-end fields in an irrigation system should be applied to the new fieldowners; that is, they should restrict their water use to periods of excess supply, particularly to the wet season. Given that the new fields lay between the water source and the old fields, ensuring compliance with court rulings was next to impossible without co-operation from new appropriators. The state reserves to itself all legitimate use of coercive force, but law enforcement in peripheral regions is inadequate to the task of patrolling irrigation systems. Needless to say, the ruling was not complied with.

Finally, the original rice-field owners threatened to obtain a new state water permit in order to demonstrate the lack of excess water above their legitimate needs. An engineer was brought in to assess the litre-per-second consumption needs of the original fields. People told us of watching this man dig holes in the streambed to time how long it took the flow to fill them and throw sticks in the water to measure the time it took them to cover a distance. This highly public display seems to have motivated the new appropriators to agree to a local solution, and a meeting was struck which resulted in a timed water-rotation schedule based on field size. The smaller, new field sections receive three hours of water per day, while the larger, original fields are watered for the rest of the day. To ensure compliance, a *man'dapis* distributes the water. This solution proved successful, and other irrigation systems within Kabayan have adopted similar procedures during the dry season. This compromise ends open conflict, but has unfortunate production consequences. Water which could irrigate rice paddies laying at lower, warmer elevations where rice does well, must be shared with owners of rice paddies at higher altitudes, where productivity is low and rice plants are often sterile. In some rocky or porous areas, water no longer reaches the original fields in sufficient quantities to enable a dry-season crop of rice. The limited water resource is being overtaxed, an unintended consequence of the above chain of events.

It is apparent that participants on both sides of the state-local divide have proceeded on the basis of an oversimplified understanding of the jural concepts of their counterparts. For example, in those disputes developing after the 1978 establishment of the village courts (*lupong*), adjudication was attempted in the lupong forum. This forum draws on the same actors as tong tongs (the respected elders) as the lupong was explicitly developed to utilize local custom and procedures. Nevertheless, the state requires that lupong decisions be forwarded to the Ministry of Local Government, and that cases brought to a higher court first be heard at this level. Silliman (1985) has discussed the implications of this requirement for local justice. Here I want to draw attention to the resulting confusion among members of the conciliation panels (*Pankat ng Tagapagkasundo*) who decide on a particular case. In Kabayan, these people often seemed confused as to what is expected of them. While the government instructs them to use local custom in resolving disputes, lupong members are also aware that cases can proceed to state courts where their decisions will receive close scrutiny. They hope that lupong decisions will be found reasonable and will be upheld. The problem is that their understanding of state legal reasoning is based solely on local gossip about previous court cases. The result is a tendency to employ a jumbled combination of local jural principles and perceived state rules. The situation is similar in the upper courts; while state courts (especially municipal and Regional Trial Courts) involve state legislation and state-trained legal professionals, they often employ state perceptions of "indigenous law" garnered from members' exposure to lupong decisions and to literature about "Igorot" culture.

Local gossip suggests that both lupong and state judicial participants have demonstrated errors in understanding. For example, many members of the state bureaucracy operate under the misconception that irrigation systems in mountain communities are communal. This mis-perception is widespread among the various government bureaus and has become self-reinforcing since it has also reached into the community. The National Irrigation Authority, for example, recognizes three types of irrigation systems: national (constructed and managed by the government), communal (constructed and managed by the farmers in a community and to which the government offers financial assistance) and private (to which the government only offers technical advice). Communal systems are supposedly run by a "legal body made up of the farmers who use the water from the communal system" (Korten and Siy 1988:2). This terminology is a reflection of the bureaucratic understanding of how indigenous systems work (ibid.:30. See also the various publications involving de los Reyes). It exacerbates the problem in Kabayan, since the widespread use of this terminology results in demands by new landholders for an equal share in all available water. The 1976 *Water Code* reinforces this interpretation since it makes the state the only legitimate owner of water with the right to grant water permits to users. It was explained to farmers that the new code would prevent individual monopolization of water. The villagers' interpretation of this legislation is that water is now a communal resource. Villagers' application of this interpretation in village court decisions has reinforced state perceptions that the Ibaloi are communal.

Villagers' behaviour has obviously been influenced. For example, in one case an irrigation system originally involving fields totalling one hectare eventually expanded to twice that size. The spring supplying the canal proved insufficient to meet this expansion, and the farmers along this system began to tap a neighbouring system's water supply. At first this was justified as a stop-gap measure, but the dwindling water supply (due to erosion and destruction of the watershed) led to increased demands, until the viability of the second system was threatened. The result was a dispute in which the old state titles were trotted out for the third time; the farmers along the first canal responded by appealing to the "communal" 1976 *Water Code*. The case was settled locally when a meeting of all concerned farmers agreed to a timed water-rotation schedule during the height of the dry season. This procedure is still followed today, uniting the field owners of two different canals into a single distribution system for a short period every year.

Meanwhile, farmers on a third irrigation system also experienced difficulties when interlopers opened small fields along their canal. This dispute involved fewer people with more limited resources, and this may explain why it was heard in a tong tong venue. As in other cases, there has been no successful resolution. Perhaps leaning on previous state decisions, the elders argued that the new landowners should only take water when there was an excess. But no one can agree on the definition of excess, and hard feelings still exist between the original and new field owners. One farmer in the same area has a different complaint. This man and his wife have property on which a perennial spring rises; in the past, the spring was used to irrigate their fields. Community officials pressured them to give up their water rights in this spring so that it could be used as a domestic water source for a section of the town. In return, they and their descendants were promised water from the above irrigation canal. Unfortunately, not all of the people affected agreed that the town had the right to so allocate "communal" water, and this couple exchanged a reliable and trouble-free source of water for one which is unreliable and which has to be shared with feuding field neighbours.

New demands on water supplies continue to develop. In the mid-1970s, Kabayan officials managed to gain provincial funds to expand irrigation facilities. The money was used to open construction on two new canals, both of which would tap water upstream from pre-existing irrigation systems. Feelings ran high over these projects. The landowners who would benefit were at odds with those who felt threatened. The former justified overruling the latter by reference to "communal" water. Meanwhile residents of sitios located near the construction expressed concern about the dangerous rock blasting involved in the construction. Some people refused to grant right-of-way for the canals to cross their land. Many felt that there was insufficient water to support two new major canals and signed a petition to have construction stopped. When the petition was brought to the Provincial Fiscal, it was suggested that the new canals draw water only in the wet season. Mindful of previous experiences with such agreements, landholders continued to press their pre-existing claims to the water. The problem was finally resolved by default, when funding proved insufficient to complete the new canals.

The question of rights in water continues to be controversial in Kabayan. A key informant made the following statement when asked who owned the water:

> The water belongs to those people who have the water right. The government asked us to renew that water right, but we said: "Why?" Really, the only reason we wanted that water right was for fear of the mines. But we have kept the old water right just to show who really owns the water. Most people here now do not recognize that water right. They say the water belongs to everyone. That water right now is only used to achieve compromise between the newer rice field owners and the older rice field owners. They had to use it because, before, people were always stealing our water! You cannot hurt them, they are your neighbours.

He went on to temper this statement:

> You must realize, here we share everything together. Even the owners of the rice fields, really, all their ownership means is that they have the right to sell that land. But we all work the rice fields together. One man cannot horde rice from the others. We have e'so here, a 50/50 sharing of the yield.

Here he appears to be making a distinction between rights of use, rights of alienation and rights of exclusion, not all of which are necessarily recognized as part of "ownership" in Kabayan.

When the farmers interviewed in the irrigation survey were asked if there was any water right for the source of their irrigation water, 69 percent said that there was such a right. A further 26 percent said that there had been such a right but it had expired. One farmer said that there was no such right, and one replied that he did not know if such a right existed. When questioned about who had the right to take water from the canals, informant responses fell into two conflicting camps. Many farmers point out that the old water right makes no difference since "it is no longer followed." They feel that all rice fields have a right to water, and some call this right "communal." The other camp claims that the way water is presently distributed is actually due to the "considerations" or "patience" of the original paddy owners; some say there is now "dealing about water" between newly constructed rice field owners and the "owners" of the water. What is clear from these comments is that various, sometimes contradictory, principles are at work regarding rights to property. This can also be demonstrated with disputes involving gold.

Gold Disputes

During the field research period, the state considered native mining illegal. This fact was openly acknowledged by interviewed miners; however, in Kabayan the gold deposit area as well as several other promising locations were sometimes spoken of as "communal" property. Individual tunnel owners were not in a position to dispute the communal designation since this might lead to someone informing on their illegal tunnelling. This situation was used to pressure elite members of the community, who financed much of the tunnel construction, to widen access to this resource.

Only two of the five gold-related disputes documented actually involved gold, while the other three involved side-effects of mine activity: potential landslides and diverting irrigation water for mine operations. For example, a number of years ago several tunnels were developed directly upslope from one Kabayan sitio. Although owners of paddies located below the mine site were concerned, good results were being achieved and the mining expanded. After a particularly violent typhoon, however, a large slide destroyed many rice fields. People blamed the slide on mine tunnelling, and community elders were able to convince the miners to shut down at that location. Similarly, when people began to mine again at Kamista's old mine site, gold washing at the site concerned people from a neighbouring community whose paddies were downslope of the washing site. Again, community elders convinced miners not to use water at the mine site. Now sacks of material from the mines are carried down the mountain over a kilometre away to a spring where they are processed and the gold extracted. The alternative was to go to court, something the miners wanted to avoid.

In the two cases which actually involved gold, dispute resolution has been more difficult. In one case, the son of the man who purchased Kamista's mine canal has threatened to get the gold mine area surveyed to see if any tunnels are located within the parcel his father purchased. His goal is to acquire a percentage of all ore taken from such tunnels. Local people are unsure of his chances of gaining state-recognized rights to such tunnels, but some have "run off" anyone suspected of being government surveyors, resulting in assault charges. Kamista also sold the old mine tunnel parcel to a lowlander, and people in the community made it impossible for this individual to visit the site and get an accurate legal description of it, guiding him instead on "wild goosechases" through the hills. The mine site subsequently changed hands again, and the second purchaser has had no better luck in finding his way to the property.

One final gold-related dispute involves an individual who bagged tailings from the gold washing site to ship off for trace metal extraction. Members of the community complained that he did not have the right to market this "communal" resource. When the problem was brought before community elders, he was required to cease his shipments until a fair method of sharing this "communal" resource could be worked out. The sacks of material sat by the side of the road for all the months of our research in the community.

Conclusions

In an atmosphere of conflicting authority systems and where manipulating the adjudication venues is a successful strategy, the wealthy often have the advantage of superior resources, allowing them to take their claim where their chances are best. This has happened in Kabayan. Wealthier claimants have won property disputes by default when poorer claimants could not afford legal representation or travel expenses to a state court. Generating the perception among poorer opponents that a case would go to state court is often enough to force them to back down. Such strategy depends on the local perception that rights defined by the state legal system are in opposition to customary practice. This perception is common in Kabayan. I did not hear of a case in which local tenure rules were said to be properly understood in any state dispute venue. But here a distinction between customary and indigenous rules is important. Some cases suggest that one party was more "creative" than the other in "inventing" differences between local and state practice; the elabouration of a communal tribal history is one example. To confuse the situation for both local people and government officials, there are also cases in which the state has demonstrated a willingness to apply its particular understanding of local rules. These cases have fuelled behaviour which has ultimately benefitted the poor. In all the cases discussed in this chapter, local perceptions had the effect of changing property relations in Kabayan, wherever the locus of dispute resolution and whatever the judicial outcome of the case.

In conclusion, if we compared the situation for land, water and gold resources in Kabayan, property rights in this community appear to have broadened over time, to the disadvantage of formerly elite members of the community. The role of legal pluralism and the resulting discrepancy in property right definition appears first to have reinforced social stratification because it was first utilized by the elite. Then, as individual strategies to manipulate the discrepancy between local and state laws began to expand, legal pluralism actually had a levelling effect on community social stratification. This is true for all three resources discussed, but for varying reasons. The case of land is the most straightforward; state tenure laws are blamed as the source of changes to local property relations. Some elders bemoan the lack of free grazing area around the community, for example, pointing to state preference for privatization as the reason such lands have all been tax-declared by individuals. In terms of water and gold, elders view the situation as a bit more complex: some blame individual greed; others point to the right everyone has to economic survival. For all three resources, however, the so-called customary, ancestral communal rights are being selectively used to support broadened access to resources.

There is another aspect of this which is important to recognize. Franz von Benda-Beckmann (1989) shows how governments use law first as the magic charm and then as the scapegoat in attempting to change behaviour through legislation. But there is also a sense in which the government perception of custom or local law generates an escape hatch for them when the success of their policies creates problems. The government in the Philippines has enacted legislation affecting the Cordillera region, and this has created property disputes which government agents in the court system are required to deal with. In many of the cases discussed in this chapter, the court system does not resolve these issues but instead pursues a policy which thrusts the problem back into the lap of local people on the grounds of their cultural difference. This policy saves the government the trouble and expense of dealing with the problems they have helped to create. However, members of local communities can sometimes benefit when this strategy simultaneously leaves room to manoeuvre in resource competition.

In order to understand the consequences of this strategy for local property systems, and the connections with social stratification, it will be necessary to look in more detail at diachronic factors at work in Kabayan over the last several centuries. But first, I will turn to questions of the resulting social groups organized around access to property (Appell's point number three from the first page of this chapter). These were the groups affected by the purposive strategies outlined in this chapter. Needless to say, it is difficult to identify the salient features of property-concerned social entities in present day Kabayan.

SIX

Modern Property Relations

Chapter Four identified a number of productive resources important to the current Kabayan economy. Chapter Five discussed the nature of historical and ongoing disputes over rights to those resources. This chapter examines the emerging social entities which struggle to control property. Furthering Appell's goal of recognizing "emergent structure" in the press of daily behaviour relies on developing a method to recognize the "reflexive event" whereby patterns of deviance become accepted as the new norm. In terms of the social entities which utilize productive resources, Appell suggests that the reflexive moment occurs when property rights become recognized as valid and reified into legal principles. However, the empirical evidence suggests that reification does not necessarily follow the establishment of behavioural norms but may rather arise from efforts to create such norms through establishment of the desired rule (see Benda-Beckmann 1989). This is as true of the "folk law" of the supposedly primitive world as it is of the "rationalized institutions" of the West. In addition, it is important to realize that such reification may *not* bring about behavioural conformity. When reification is a strategy pursued by competing interests, the opportunity for the generation of structure is tempered by the perversity of individuals in their selection of behaviour options. This chapter demonstrates the resulting problems for social theorists who hope to identify structure. It re-examines the applicability of concepts such as communal, corporate and private property by relating these concepts to emerging, past or present social entities in Kabayan.

I begin this analysis with the largest social unit (the community) and progress through to smaller property-holding units to demonstrate the similarities and differences which exist between Ibaloi and Western concepts of property holding and to show the questionable applicability of terms often applied in the ongoing contrast between the West and non-West. The chapter concludes with the argument that the consequences of group and individual strategies are enormous, and that they are not planned outcomes. Purposive strategies have an effect on structure that cannot be predicted, and benefits (as the disputes in Chapter Five demonstrate) may accrue in unexpected quarters. Chapter Seven goes on to orient the reader to the flow of events in Kabayan to gain a better understanding of these unexpected outcomes and beneficiaries.

Part One: Communal Uplands?

People in Kabayan identified several resources, including forests, irrigation systems, gold deposits, pasture and virgin lands, as "communal." However, the anthropological literature on communal groups discussed in Chapter Two contrasts sharply with the situation in Kabayan. Both contrast with recent literature on "common pool resources" (see especially Ostrom 1990).

As one informant explained it:

> "*Muyong*," that is the term used in Buguias [a community to the north of Kabayan] to refer to what we now call "communal" [as in communal forest]. We never had that word here. That "muyong" means that everyone can own it as one—they are entitled to use it as one. In Kabayan we only use that borrowed term "communal."

One elderly man remembered what he thought was a corresponding Ibaloi term, *bodusan,* "free for use by everyone." However, as I will demonstrate in the following discussion, this is quite a different concept, and the confusion between these differing concepts has had interesting consequences for the formation of property-holding groups in Kabayan.

In Kabayan, many resources are exploited in an individual, opportunistic manner, including wild animals and plants, fish in streams and rivers, forest products, grasslands for pasture and roof thatch, alluvial gold deposits and hillside areas for swidden fields. The rights people have to these resources are based on the fact that no one else got to them first. If pressed on the source of these rights, elders speak of "ancestral" heritage. The reference is to rights enjoyed equally by all members of a community. Bromley (1989:204) calls these "open access" resources and concludes that these are not a form of property. Van Vollenhoven, however, calls a similar concept under Indonesian *adat* law, community "rights of allocation" (see Burns 1989:8-10), and views it as an inalienable right held in common. If the Ibaloi practised this right of allocation, it may have been translated into the English language as "communal."

While such rights of allocation could be viewed as a form of communal property, it appears there are significant differences when compared to common property rights as described in the theoretical literature such as Berkes 1989, Bromley 1989, Grossi 1981, Maine 1890, Ostrom 1990 and Wade 1987, and in the ethnographic literature such as Brush 1977, Glick 1970,

Lewis 1971 and Halperin 1988. One criterion which has been used to distinguish communal institutions from other arrangements is the degree of definition to membership boundaries (Ostrom 1990:91). "Open access" institutions cannot close off access to "outsiders," whereas communal institutions
have clearly demarcated boundaries which allow them to do so. By this criterion, the right of allocation appears to be a communal right.

For example, Ibaloi historical data suggest that the council of elders in
any one community exercised some authority over some resources. Access
within the community was based on a "first come, first served" principle,
but in cases involving external users, the elders intervened. For example, a
century ago water was plentiful in Kabayan Poblacion and when people from
a neighbouring community wished to develop rice paddies using a spring rising within Kabayan boundaries, they approached Kabayan elders to gain permission. An agreement was reached and notarized with a public feast for
which the people of the neighbouring community provided the pigs and
carabaos. A canal several kilometres long was constructed to supply the
rice terraces, and even in the present-day situation of water scarcity the
agreement is respected. This event reflects what Van Vollenhoven recognizes as a common principle in rights of allocation; that is, in consideration of a tribute or fee, the community agrees to allow outsiders access to
community resources (Burns 1989: 10).[1] Elders negotiated these tributes
as representatives of the right-bearing body, that is, the community. Further, the elders enforced restrictions on alienation, again in reference to
outsiders.

However, Ostrom (1990:91-102) lists several other criteria important to
successful, sustainable "common pool resource" institutions. These include:
(1) appropriation rules consistent with local conditions, (2) participation by
appropriators in modification of appropriation rules, (3) monitoring of
appropriators, (4) graduated sanctions to prevent abuses, (5) conflict-resolu-
tion mechanisms which are accessible, low-cost and local, (6) minimal recognition of the right to organize, including the right to develop rules and,
finally, (7) nested enterprises with component parts in an integrated structure.
There are no social institutions currently operating in Kabayan that fit these
criteria, as I will demonstrate with several examples. Presently, the use of
resources on a "first come, first served" basis continues in Kabayan, although the number of resources treated in this fashion has declined and
become more contentious. Indeed, when the word communal is used in refer-

---

1   More evidence for this same authority of allocation appears in Fray Antolin's
    journals, which document gold-mining communities making contracts with neigh-
    bouring communities to pasture cattle (Scott 1974:146-56).

ence to resources, it is the signal of significant conflict and of a particular strategy of competition. While this strategy was explored in the last chapter, here I discuss the groups affected by the conflict and its outcome.

Forest

Forested areas near Kabayan are an important resource, providing building materials and fuel, among other products. Every community member has an equal right to gather products required for domestic purposes from anywhere within these forests. However, there are disagreements over the boundaries of the communal forest and over the definition of membership in the community. The Ibaloi define both quite differently from the state. For the state, community membership is based on residence, or on paying municipal taxes, owning land or opening a business within the community. For the Ibaloi, membership in the community depends on birthright, descent from past or present members of the community or an affinal alliance. As a consequence of this state-local disagreement, many people today take forest resources, whether or not they meet local membership rules. The people of Kabayan can do little to prevent use and abuse of forests in their area by either external or internal users.

There are three reasons for this, all related to political incorporation. First, according to state law, land within Kabayan boundaries is of two types: private and public.[2] Access to public land is limited by government regulation. Second, the Philippine government does not recognize the indigenous boundaries of the community, which historically encompassed present-day Kabayan and a neighbouring barangay. These two communities are now divided for administrative purposes. Third, the state determines membership in any Philippine community by reference to residence, for purposes of taxation and of voter registration and not on ethnicity or kinship connections.

While the state has granted a portion of the public lands within the community boundaries to be used as a communal forest, none of the above criteria Ostrom identifies applies to the community in regards to the management of this forest. Any person who is legally a resident of Kabayan has the right to collect forest products for private use from the communal forest; commercial exploitation is not allowed by local people. Branches and deadfall may be freely collected, but residents need a permit from the Bureau of Forest Development to cut down a living tree. Local input is not solicited on management or rule-making. The state view of the scarce good, the social entity connected to it and the rights members of that social entity have in the

---

2   I have already discussed the fact that local people often do not accept the state's designation of some lands as public.

scarce good are all very different from Ibaloi conceptions. The community does not fit the criteria Ostrom identifies as important to sustainable communal institutions. This situation has proven to be a severe handicap to local people.

For example, the Philippine government granted a large tract of public lands in the Kabayan region to a commercial corporation which extensively logged the slopes above Kabayan Poblacion over the last several decades. Local people did not accept the state's right to determine access to forest products within their community boundaries and resented the erosion and watershed deterioration that resulted from logging. Consequently, state rules were not well conformed with and the company found it difficult to protect their lumber concession from local appropriators. The company tried hiring forest guards from the community. One such man told me:

> I think it was 1970 when Bobok opened their logging around here. They asked for somebody who is respected in the town to be their forest guard. They told me that the people should just take the branches [for fuel]. But they must not take all [the tree]. I told them: "Alright. But what about the houses?" They advised me to ask the people to get a permit [to cut house timbers]. Of course, I said yes, but wherever I wasn't, the people would just cut and cut. It was hard for me.

This hiring policy obviously created friction in the community and was not very successful in limiting local appropriation.

Other uses made of public lands have infringed on local control and use of resources and have increased community heterogeneity, both problems for common property management (see Ostrom 1990:89). When outsiders make improvements, the land can be registered for tax declaration. Immigrants from other regions make use of this provision by creating swidden fields and settling within traditional Kabayan boundaries. Such people are not tied into the community through common kinship, religious belief or traditional law. There are no effective sanctions controlling their behaviour or their appropriation of resources such as forests, water, land and gold. Given these sorts of problems, it is difficult to recognize a communal social entity operating relative to forest resources or to land in Kabayan, although such entities may have been viable in the past.

Water

As Chapter Five demonstrates, a second example of a so-called communal resource is water, especially water involved in irrigation. The membership requirements and rules of use rights in water and in irrigation systems can be discussed for two distinct levels. The first is the communitywide level, concerned with water in general, which is discussed in this section. The second level is the individual irrigation canals and their infrastructure, rice paddies and water supplies, which I reserve for later discussion.

When we first arrived in the community, the mayor expressed the opinion that

> We have communal irrigation here. The government has never touched it. It is our life's blood and a crier only has to shout from the mountain top that there would be irrigation damage and people from all around this place would rush to assist.

Further investigation found that irrigation in Kabayan actually represents a very complex case of property rights (see Chapters Four and Five). Non-residents of Kabayan can be members of a Kabayan irrigation system whenever they own irrigated land in the community. Some people draw water from canal systems where they are not members, and in general, there is no neat overlap between community and irrigation system.

But some locals argue that irrigation water is a communal resource, since the majority of community households gain economic benefit from irrigation. There is an acknowledged "community of interest" in the protection of water, the resource which makes irrigation possible; in the past, uplands communities have gone to war over water. Other factors contribute to the local perception of water in Kabayan as a communal resource, including the dry-season land-preparation rotation of available water supplies between the various irrigation systems and the elders' reluctance to totally refuse anyone water even as a sanction to protect rights of first appropriation. These factors suggest that the community is beginning to view water as an important resource which cannot be monopolized for the benefit of the few at the expense of the many.

As with forest resources, the state view is different. According to government law, no formal water rights currently exist to protect Kabayan water sources from external threats or from internal competition. The state *might* recognize what Appell terms a jural aggregate; prior appropriators are recognized in the new code as having the strongest claim to a formal water permit. At the least, the state mis-perception of mountain communities as communal entities might provide some protection from external threats. Most people are confident that their long agricultural use of water sources provides the necessary legal basis for protection, even under state law. However, as Chapter Five demonstrates, there is little or no community consensus today on the best use to which the limited resources of water should be put. Some people view the use of water for gold washing as a high priority, although this is presently a minority view. Nevertheless, as long as there is support for labelling water rights as "communal" without corresponding social institutions to manage such a resource, such views will be hard to reject. This, in fact, may be the archetypical "tragedy of the commons," but it does not relate to indigenous communalism nor to any inherent characteristic of a common pool resource (see Ostrom 1990:14).

Gold

According to some people, gold deposits are another communal resource. Here, as with water, forests and land, a community right of allocation existed in the past. There is historical evidence that communities along the Agno River valley, including Kabayan, restricted outsider access to their gold deposit areas (Scott 1974:149). The same historical sources suggest that panning in rivers and streams was also restricted to community members at some locations. In present-day Kabayan, "communal" gold sites are said to include various locations on the slopes of Mount Al-Al and certain alluvial deposits along various streams and the river. Some people say that these sites are communal because every community member has an equal right to work in undeveloped areas of the sites. However, as with other resources, there are complications.

Ibaloi indigenous law granted an individual liberal-style ownership rights in an improved portion of a gold-deposit site. The investment of labour to create a mine tunnel lifted the site from the realm of open access and restricted appropriation to the developer(s). Long-term tenure was created similar to that held in rice paddies. However, unlike rice paddies, mines could not be subdivided and worked individually; consequently, devolution rules favoured individual sons. Further, working a mine involves large numbers of people. Once slavery was outlawed under the American administration, the operation of mines began to resemble irrigation canals more than they did rice paddies. That is to say, several levels of involvement in tunnels complicated the picture.

Unlike forest products, which are exploited by individuals or domestic family units, the resources of gold and water have historically involved extra-domestic groups, the members of which labour to create, manage and benefit from irrigation systems and gold mines. But there is no evidence to suggest that a communal form of property was involved in the exploitation of water or gold. In the past, builders created and managed tunnels and irrigated field systems with slave labour. The level of investment determined individual member shares in the benefits. As the next section of this chapter suggests, these groups resembled corporate more than communal groups. But here, too, the discrepancy between indigenous and state property law has had an effect over time. In both tunnels and irrigation canals, there are now providers, producers and appropriators—which are not always the same individuals. I argue that this has had much to do with the rise of "communal" property concepts and their application to resources such as gold and water in Kabayan. "Inventing" a communal background is a strategy which attacks indigenous property-holding group rights in resources. In order to substantiate this argument, I will next examine indigenous ideas about corporate-style property-holding social entities and contrast those ideas with the current operation of such entities.

Part Two: Corporate Entities?

As Chapter Two indicates, the concept of the corporation is as complicated as that of communal groups, with a similar wealth of theoretical and ethnographic literature. The distinction between the two concepts is subtle but important, as Appell's (1976) work demonstrates. Communal property is held in common, corporate property is held in severalty. In communal groups, appropriators can make demands equal to other appropriators; in corporate groups, shares in the property are variable and often proportionate to status (sometimes genealogy-based) in the group. Individual shares are often alienable and devolvable at will. The blurring of these distinctions is one problem with Ostrom's (1990) discussion of examples of common-pool resource institutions. A useful contrast in this regard is provided by Berkes and Farvar (1989:9), who want to separate the common resource itself from the "property-rights regime" under which it is held, of which there are several types. The following discussion demonstrates that although corporate-like "property-rights regimes" existed in Ibaloi society, few of them were based on kinship principles and even fewer are functioning without problems today. One entity that was clearly kin-based and corporate (the bunak), no longer functions in the same way. The organization of irrigation is a good example of former structural arrangements and of current corporate organizational problems.

Irrigation Canals

To the casual observer, the number of independent systems involved in irrigation in Kabayan is not apparent. An impression of communal irrigation is reinforced by local comments. When questioned about the antiquity of various canals or field sections, for example, people maintain that the entire system was built many generations ago and that no part is older than any other. But when irrigation organization and conflict is investigated, a picture of several discrete irrigation entities begins to emerge. There has never been a communitywide response to threats to tenure in the agricultural water supply; farmers in Kabayan have never united to obtain state water title. Narratives of irrigation disputes demonstrate that different canals are thought to represent different entities as a result of separate histories. Once again, local interpretations contrast with the government view. I examine indigenous irrigation law first and the social entities it acknowledged.

Historically, water rights were based on precedence; those who developed irrigated land created exclusive tenure in the water from the source to point of exit from their system. Under indigenous rules, any spring rising on land which an individual has established rights in is considered the property of the owner until the water flows off the property. If the water is used to irrigate rice terraces, the spring, the irrigation canals and the rice paddies all become individually held property, subject to the indigenous laws of devolution. Excess water which flows away from the developed lands, however, remains an open resource. While a few irrigation canals in Kabayan were developed from isolated springs, by single individuals, the majority were not. This brings us to riparian water rights under indigenous law, and to the social groups connected with irrigation.

Irrigation in Kabayan relies on diversion weirs which divert water from a stream into a canal system. In the past, irrigation canals were developed using the contributions of those who planned to create paddies with the water. Contributions were rarely equal; those members of the group who were able, contributed more construction materials, more animals to feed the workers and, in the past, more slave labour towards the canal construction. Only elite families could afford the expense of extensive canal and terrace development. Water allocation, once the system was constructed, was proportionate to the individual investment. Since some members of a co-operative group contributed more to the construction costs, they received the right to more water, and thus were able to open and develop more paddy lands. Subsequently, the proportionate division of the water on the basis of paddy size has remained a stable principle in these irrigation groups. The lands developed into paddies were individual holdings, but the irrigation infrastructure remained an indivisible, group-held unit. As such, the canal devolved to the group of people inheriting land from the original constructing group. Many of these people have kinship connections in common, but kin ties do not organize the group. The irrigation infrastructure is held as property by the membership, while the land (and the water rights bundled with the land) is divided and redivided each generation, thus increasing the number of owners in the irrigation group.

These indigenous irrigation groups held the right to first access to water from the system source, based on prior appropriation. The group of landowners along one system were recognized as a property-holding unit under indigenous law, and one among them represented their interests in any conflict involving another irrigation group or other potential users of their water. The group as a whole maintained the infrastructure with co-operative labour, but this did not change the partition of water. While the individual members of

the group were subject to the majority decisions reached by the group in relation to structure maintenance and conflict resolution, the owners of wider
lands within the system carried more weight in decision-making. Conflicts
arising among the members of an irrigation group were mediated by and
resolved with the help of such "elite" members.

Under indigenous practices, conflict could and often did arise, either
between groups or when the boundaries between the original paddies and
more recently constructed paddies were disputed. However in the indigenous
setting, rules adapted to local situations, plus ritual and land-tenure practices,
social stratification, power and prestige, worked to limit or to resolve such
conflicts when they arose. The numbers of members in irrigation groups was
smaller, and status hierarchies limited open disputes. Various mechanisms
allowed owners of irrigated lands to prevent the opening of new fields near
their canals. Such groups owned the infrastructure as a common resource
while dividing the water in severalty among them. A canal-based group was a
well-recognized social entity which Appell would term a jural collectivity.
These entities also correspond to many characteristics of the corporate group
as defined in Chapter Two. It is interesting to note that Ostrom (1990) treats
an equally complex lowlands Filipino irrigation system as a communal entity,
a classification Lewis (1991) would refute.

The analysis is complicated by the fact that the Philippine state has a different definition for legally recognized irrigation groups. First, the members
of the irrigating group must form an association formerly chartered under
state law. Second, under the present (post-1976) legislation, all water
resources in the country belong to the state and are administered by the
National Water Resources Council. In order that rights of appropriation be
enforceable under state law, a water permit must be obtained, whether or not
the water rises on private property. This permit may be granted to individual
legal citizens, or to "juridical persons who are duly qualified by law to
exploit and develop water," that is, state-recognized irrigators' associations
in the case of agricultural use (*Philippines Today*:43). No formal irrigation
associations exist in Kabayan, and no water permits have been obtained;
according to the state, a property-holding group concerned with water does
not exist in Kabayan. This would make the canal-based group a jural aggregate in Appell's terminology. This is a useful designation, since state law
does not admit the existence of a property-holding group, and yet a group of
people sharing a resource does exist.

However, at least two irrigation groups *did* seek and (perhaps) received
state-recognized water tenure in the past. Prior to 1976, the state recognized
two kinds of water ownership, public dominion and private ownership. Privately owned waters were those which fell on, rose within, were contained by

or found under privately tenured lands, so long as the water remained on that land (ibid.:38). It is doubtful that the water title granted to the two Kabayan groups fell under this type of tenure. Waters which were found in areas of public domain were, likewise, part of the public domain. Claims to water from public domain sources were granted in the forms of concessions which were usually awarded by prescription for 10 years. Both private and concession water tenure was "without prejudice to third persons" (ibid.:39); that is, one person or group could not use the water to the detriment of others downstream who also benefitted from the water. It is probable that the Kabayan canal-based groups obtained a water concession.

Local people claim that government titles to water were granted to two separate groups; in other words, titles were likely given to the same groups as those recognized by community elders under indigenous law. Present-day owners of these two canals are aware that their state tenure has lapsed under new regulations. Those interviewed about this development felt that there was no need to get a new water permit since the old ones prove first appropriation and prior right to the water, even under the new laws. Officials in the National Irrigation Authority offices agreed, but made two provisos: first appropriation provides some protection against challenges but this is at the discretion of state officials. Also, as with forest stands, the present tendency in state recognition of water tenure is to emphasize group needs over individual water users. Rules of membership and of incorporating new members, as well as devolution of the property, may not be acknowledged by the government as they are by local people. According to Appell, the local group, with less than full state recognition, might be termed a jural aggregate to distinguish it from those with full state recognition (a jural collectivity). Ostrom (1990) on the other hand would lump all such groups together under the term communal. It should be obvious by now that depending on what jural system is used to define the property rights, different terms could variously be applied to the same property-holding group. Our terminology is not yet sufficiently sophisticated to encompass real-life complexities.

Gold Tunnels

In the gold resources of Kabayan Poblacion, we find yet another example of the complexity of Ibaloi property relations. One aspect of this complexity is the way in which the Ibaloi have tried to balance the rights of all community members to access to productive resources with the rights of individuals or groups who invest labour to develop these resources. As with water, there is a communitywide interest in the resources of the gold-deposit areas, and anyone who is a member of the community has the right to work undeveloped areas within these sites or to pan in adjacent streambeds in the rainy season.

However, like the irrigation and the land-holding system, Ibaloi indigenous law has undergone severe transformations.

Today individual tunnels at several gold deposit areas are owned by individuals or small groups. The developer(s) of a tunnel may be an individual, a married couple, a group of siblings or of friends and/or relatives. In the past, these gold tunnels were developed by a single family with the assistance of slave labourers (see Scott 1974:151 and 184). In the present day, tunnel-operating groups are composed of several co-owners and many temporary workers. Founder's rights in tunnels are not lost if work in the tunnel stops. Control over the tunnel and yield is not always retained by the founding member(s), however, if it is kept in operation with the labour of non-member workers. In late May 1984, although approximately 20 tunnels existed at the site, only three of them were in production, and all were worker managed. The other tunnels were secured with gates. Tunnel founders *were* recognized in indigenous law as property-holding units. Today the eldest member of the managing group is group representative and is held responsible by community elders with respect to the operations of that tunnel. Since destructive landslides and deaths through tunnel collapse have occurred, the locked gates may reflect safety and liability under indigenous rules as much as the desire to restrict non-owner access.

Operating tunnels are worked by small shifts of three to four men. All the material that is extracted on any one shift (the *nava*) is equally divided among the workers on that shift and whatever gold is found in their share constitutes the miners' wage. The owners of some tunnels receive a share of the material only on the shifts which they personally work. Others take a share of all nava extracted. The difference may depend on the extent and type of work required to make the tunnel productive. If workers are required to cut timber for supports, extend tunnels and reinforce them, then expertise in the form of retired commercial miners may be required. A miners' association has been formed by these men (the Shallow Miners' Association), and they have taken over the operation of some mines. In such cases, the owners have even given up the right to control access to their tunnel. From the perspective of the locals, a property-owning entity exists for each tunnel; however, locals dispute whether ownership rests with an individual, corporate-style or communal group. State law, of course, takes the government view of mineral rights. This may be the real reason that tunnel owners have difficulty restricting access to the profits of the tunnel.

According to informants, including the eldest miner at the mine site, there is no state-recognized title to the mine site vested in the community, or in any of the individual tunnel-owning groups: "this is not a registered mine. We are here as what they call 'hide leaders' because [the mines] are against the Philippine Government [law]. This is not a registered mine so we are very silent about this.'' One of the difficulties in registering any mining claim in that particular tunnel area is that a pre-existing state title exists for the land, a result of the mining boom in the 1930s. Thus, the state view is that there is a single legal owner for the mine site, which is private property. This goes a long way towards explaining the success of the Shallow Miners' Association, which has operated in a way to undermine the property rights granted under indigenous laws.

The association has several guiding members who have commercial mining experience and a larger component which pays a small membership fee in contribution towards accident benefits and legal fees in case of litigation against illegal mining. This association has a president, a vice-president and a treasurer who are elected from the general membership. The members in the association include some tunnel owners, as well as young men from the community who do not have an interest in any one tunnel but who rely on association membership to gain them entrance to working shifts. Because this miners' association presents a united front for the protection of miners' interests in the site, the eldest members have been recognized by the elders of the community and by the state as representatives of all miners in disputes involving irrigation water, possible land slides and mine safety. These mining elders have been made responsible for making sure that irrigation water is not diverted for gold washing in the dry season, that tunnels are not started on unstable slopes which might slide, that young men do not work in tunnels without proper timber supports, and that live trees are not cut for timber props. The leaders of the Kabayan miners' association and others like it have made representation to the Provincial Attorney's office on the miners' behalf to gain state recognition for native mining activities. Their position versus the rights of tunnel-founders is strengthened by the fact that the state-acknowledged private ownership of the site presents a common danger to all currently involved in mining there. Here, again, it is difficult to find terminology which adequately describes the type of property group that is represented in current mining practice.

Part Three: Private Property?

In indigenous law, only gold mines and rice paddies were held by individuals and devolved to individuals, although in both cases there were residual rights lodged in a group. What is interesting in this regard is the manner in which local practice and government law have adapted to each other. The implementation of tax registration, for example, accommodates the local expectation that inherited lands are held in trust for the next generation and restricted in terms of devolution and sale. Thus people prefer to keep a wife's inherited rice fields under separate tax registration from those of her husband despite the fact that the basic economic unit of production and consumption is the nuclear household. Once children are born, such land is often registered in the name of the eldest child, who can then become administrator of the family property after the parents' death. These practices suggest that state tenure can accommodate the local fact that even rice paddies have multiple levels of rights involved in them.

But problem areas remain, particularly as involves the type of social entity connected with the property, the rights conferred in property and the rules of devolution. For example, the government holds that private property must be devolved equally to all legitimate heirs. Indigenous law also requires that all heirs inherit, but not necessarily that all heirs inherit equally. With different types of property, devolution tends to operate in different ways. In Kabayan there is a strong sense in which inherited lands are given in trust to a single owner in any one generation. Past and future generations of the bunak are held to have a continuing interest in the land. Alienation of land outside the bunak boundaries is considered calamitous; the bad caretaker who does this is thereby made a "notorious person." Of course, state law recognizes no such limitations on the rights of the individual holding private property; this has caused problems.

Further, under indigenous law, the entire bunak operated as an active property-holding entity. As has been discussed, lands which were subject to short-term productive changes were treated as the property of the individual(s) concerned until such time as the improvements were allowed to lapse (a pattern which Van Vollenhoven called "preferential rights"; see Burns 1989:33). However, in sharp contrast with the concept of preferential rights, some Cordilleran tribal groups allow for the devolution of usufruct rights to subsequent descendants. Dryland fields, pastures, woodlots and even fishing weirs are sometimes inherited in common by all the descendants of the pioneering couple. Access to the resources on such lands depends on membership in the descent group (see Wiber and Prill-Brett 1988). Attempts to accommodate bunak rights in state tenure systems may have resulted in the "block titles" so common in the uplands. Under the influence of increasing population pressure and state requirements for individual property tenure, individuals have begun to tax register such dryland, pasture and even forested areas. This, too, has created conflicts.

The state discourages any sort of accommodation to indigenous laws which give tenure in land to groups of individuals, often for practical reasons. The Kabayan tax assessor, for example, cited the frequency of disputes created by block titles. Consequently, when he registers inherited land for tax documentation, he discourages group title and presses for a division among the heirs. He argues that this is preferable, since the property-holding unit may not agree on resource distribution in subsequent years (see Chapter Five for examples). The effect of government registration of lands is to limit the rights of the bunak, while strengthening the rights of the present incumbent—even over the rights of his/her children. This is a recognized effect of the operation of the state system of land tenure: "The Torrens system has been continuously used as a device to guarantee untrammelled [*sic*] exercise of the rights of the individual owners" (Aranal-Sereno and Libarios 1983:433). The Torrens system also facilitates the transfer of property between current owners. This has the effect of commoditizing land (ibid.:432); rights in the land do not depend on use or occupation, but only on what the title supports. The paper title can easily be transferred without the owners ever actually setting foot on the property.

In the Ibaloi situation, land-grabbing resulted from the introduction of a system wherein "the ultimate proof as to the ownership and description of the land is immediately revealed on the certificate, precluding any other unknown or undeclared claim" (ibid.:432). This certificate is guaranteed by the state, and "unknown or undeclared claims" usually comprise indigenous rights. To acquire developed property, a person with the knowledge and resources had only to acquire a Torrens title to the land in question. Here, again, because the social entity (the right and duty-bearing unit in respect to property) is defined differently by local and by state jural systems, disputes have escalated. Land-grabbing escalated because the Torrens system was introduced in Benguet Province with few of the necessary bureaucratic and administrative apparatus needed to make it effective, a situation which still prevails today. The tax assessor in Kabayan frankly despaired of ever solving the problems created by the state titling system, with no current land surveys for the bulk of the Cordillera region. Recent attempts to provide adequate surveys have been underfunded and hampered by bureaucratic incompetence. This would not be such a problem were it not for the increasing treatment of land as a commodity. As the tax assessor pointed out:

> One reason there are lots of land cases now is because of loans. Previously, when the banks did not give any loans or when they did not use land as collateral, there were less land disputes. More borrowing—more disputes. And the lupong [town court] is not allowed to settle these disputes. If there are problems, it has to go to the higher court. The lupong will probably not be able to solve it. If the bank forecloses on a certain piece of property, the bank will place it in the hands of a lawyer, to order the foreclosure. It has to go through a certain [state] court.

In this way, the land and the jural rights associated with it become subject to state jural concepts, not local practice. In such situations, the state tenure of individuals is always given supremacy over the interests of the domestic or wider kinship circle.

Conclusions

This chapter has discussed patterns of property rights in Kabayan productive resources, and their allocation to social entities within Kabayan society (and beyond into Philippine society). Employing Appell's methodological approach, rights to land, forests, water and gold deposits were found to exist on many levels (primary, secondary, residual). But, Appell's and indeed anthropological terminology in general, was found to be insufficiently sophisticated to describe the various and complex kinds of social entities associated with those rights. This was especially true in reference to the indigenous setting, where property rights were lodged at the individual, kin-based corporate group, non-kin-based corporate group and communitywide level. The introduction of government tenure laws, together with state legislation regarding public lands, fit with some local entities, required accommodation of others and invented, strengthened or weakened still others. The result is an extremely fluid situation in which individual strategies are often at odds with the existence of such property-controlling social entities.

Several important points can now be made. First, there is no evidence for a "primitive" or simple level of property organization at the indigenous level, nor for a simplistic correlation between kinship and property. The historical documentation supports this, and the complex convolutions which followed political incorporation by the state also are supportive. It is important to recognize that changes occurred not only at the level of competing jural systems (political incorporation) but also followed on innovations in productive property-use patterns—a fact tied to economic integration and local responses to that process.

The economic innovations were based on individual strategies to gain or protect access to resources. Sometimes groups formed out of common interest, but these have always been cross-cut by kinship and alliance ties. Further, the strategies have not dictated planned outcomes. Behavioural choices have their own trajectory within the social sphere—a trajectory which could not have been predicted and with consequences that were in many cases surprising. In order to better understand this outcome, it is necessary to place those processes which affect property systems in context and to examine their connection to "emergent structure."

SEVEN

Getting Things Straight: Demystifying Property Relations

The previous chapters examined various resources and numerous property-holding entities of Kabayan, as well as a number of disputes concerning them. However, to understand the Kabayan situation fully, several issues relating to the analysis of property relations also have to be considered. The first issue concerns the impact of historical processes of political incorporation and economic integration on local populations. In fact, the state attempted to use law as a tool to further political incorporation. However, it is evident that for purposes of social engineering, law is a tool difficult to control (see also Benda-Beckmann 1989). In Kabayan, multiple jural levels developed and affected property relations in unpredictable ways. That unpredictability relates to the second issue, which is the utilization of legal pluralism in the strategies of economic innovators, which in turn raises the question of cultural heterogeneity and the source of variation in individual economic and political strategies. The role of individuals such as Kamista and Dukat in transforming Ibaloi society points to the importance of putting local responses to political incorporation and economic integration in context. That, in turn, requires answering questions about control over resources, the complexity of rules for allocating resources among property-holding entities, recruitment of members to and maintenance of boundaries for property-holding groups, and how these rules change. The competing claims to property in Kabayan have been the catalyst for transformations in social structure.

In this chapter, the process encompassing the interaction of the above factors will be explored, as well as the unforeseen consequences of that process. This requires re-examining some historical information presented in Chapter Three, to show how decisions taken by historical figures had an impact on the property system and relies on three sources of information: the examination of historical documents; interviews with Kabayan elders for a folk history perspective; and a comparison of the Ibaloi with neighbouring ethnic groups.

These sources of information allow for a diachronic view of the Ibaloi property system, which brings many heretofore neglected factors into focus,
including the nature of the contrasting jural orders operating in Kabayan; the
question of the beneficiaries of legal pluralism; and, the issue of cultural heterogeneity and of sources of alternative individual strategies. The chapter
concludes by investigating present directions, including the rise of communalism in modern political and economic strategies.

Part One: Legal Pluralism and Property Relations

The relevance of jural issues to property relations cannot be over-stressed. As
Sonius (1963:23) points out "the word ownership alone tells us nothing about
the owner's actual powers: only the statutes and regulations of each nation or
state can show us how far these powers reach." Barnes (1969) asks, what
happens in a polity if there are two or more centres of authority, or at least of
power, each vying for exclusive control? Such situations invariably involve a
disruption of property relations. Regulations concerning property use and
transfer within a minority culture, for example, are usually ignored or super-
seded by the jural authority of a colonial administration (see Burman and
Harrell-Bond 1979, Lam 1983, Woodman 1983). As development schemes
reach isolated regions of modern nation states, the same scenario repeats itself (see Bell 1983, Dagmar 1983, Morse 1984, Tonkinson 1983). The re-
course for a few minority populations has been militant resistance, as in the
Philippine Cordillera Central in response to the Chico River hydroelectric
development project and the Cellophil Corporation concession (see Aranal-
Sereno and Libarios 1983:445 and Prill-Brett 1985:16-17).

Problems of jurisprudence and of legitimacy under legal pluralism in the
peasant or colonial setting have received significant attention (see, for example, Barnes 1969, Benda-Beckmann 1979, Nader and Metzger 1963, Pospisil 1958, Roberts 1985, Rodman 1982, 1985, Santos 1982, and the proceedings of the 1983 and 1990 Symposia of the Commission on Folk Law and
Legal Pluralism). Many studies link the operation of competing judicial systems to the struggle over power (see especially Barnes 1969:101), but few
studies explicitly explore the consequences for property relations (for exceptions see Benda-Beckmann 1979:362-65 and Rodman 1984). There is a corresponding difficulty in understanding property-system transformations,
especially in the non-Western context. One impediment to research on the
connection between law and property is the problem of defining law. Comparative studies of non-Western and Western legal systems are based on the
Western view that "proper" law is a blind, impartial authority imposing
order in human societies (see Collins 1982:1). In this regard, there is a widespread Western perception that non-Western or "customary" law is signifi-

cantly different from "rationalized" Western law. Two tendencies exist; one is to see non-Western law as more equitable and less subject to political manoeuvring and the other is to view it as *less* equitable, perhaps less "evolved," and certainly less rational. These viewpoints spring from a Western "fetishism of law" (ibid.:10).

Legal fetishism arises from three working assumptions: (1) that a "legal order is necessary for social order," (2) that the law is a unique monolithic phenomenon which can be the focus of discrete study and (3) that law constrains equally the powerful and the weak (ibid.:11-12). Appell (1976) is guilty of "legal fetishism" when he argues that law establishes the empirical validity of a social entity which is a right and duty-bearing unit in respect to property. Appell argues further that law delineates the structure of property-holding groups. If the social entity comprises more than one member, the combined rights over property are an attribute of their jural personality. The members are seen in law as standing in a special legal relationship one to the other, a relationship which determines (or is determined by) the organization of the group. This approach misleads in two fundamental ways: first, by suggesting that it makes no difference whether the social entity concerned with property is large or small, powerful or powerless, and second, by ignoring the discrepancy between the rules and how the game is actually played. I do not believe that the sanctity of the law can be taken for granted. One reason for this is that there is no social context in which a plurality of normative orders does not exist (see Vanderlinden 1989).

Barnes (1969) accepts the existence of such plurality and acknowledges the implications for social process when he argues that we must drop the notion that legality depends on a political consensus of opinion and that the courts merely act on that consensus. He views society as normatively segmented and rival courts as instruments in the struggle for power. The structural implications are suggested by Pospisil's (1971:274) comment that: "In any society the legal rules concerned with land tenure are the most important, after laws of inheritance, with respect to social structure." Thus, the courts are the instrumentalities employed in the struggle to control productive property and ultimately the structure of society.

In pluralistic societies, interest groups arise which find it politically and/or economically advantageous to employ discrepancies between two or more competing jural systems. In such situations, as F. von Benda-Beckmann (1983) points out, jural pluralism may actually be continually reconstructed to meet the purposes of interest groups, creating what he calls a "jural jungle." Vanderlinden (1989) argues that people are influenced by different legal conceptions and use these conceptions in purposive strategies. In this chapter, I demonstrate that a single jural system was not beneficial for some segments of Ibaloi society. Some people misrepresented indigenous law to claim rights in property, to gain state title and to thus extinguish the equal or superior claim of others. But law is a tool in the hands of *all* social actors (see F. von Benda-Beckmann 1983). The advantages of legal pluralism were recognized by many different kinds of people in Ibaloi society. While unintended consequences make it difficult to control the benefits of purposive strategies involving legal pluralism, the way that individual social actors used this tool tells us a great deal about processes affecting Ibaloi property systems. Understanding these processes is vital to Appell's goal of pinpointing ''emergent'' structures in society.

D.E. Brown (1984:814) raises legal pluralism in his critique of Appell's approach, to which Appell (1984:815-17) replies: ''I do not see what analytical advantage is gained by referring to the universal processes of order and dispute resolution found in every social grouping as law.'' Appell is part of a school which defines law quite narrowly (see the interview of Pospisil in Strouthes 1990). But the legitimate problem raised by Brown does have analytical advantage, most obviously in understanding the consequences of political incorporation. In the Cordillera Central, ethnic communities of the Bontok, Ifugao, Kalinga and others are aware that state law is used to undermine their community jurisdiction and indigenous property systems. The Ibaloi are not alone in trying to deal with the intrusion of the state politico-jural system. We cannot understand these property systems without exploring political incorporation and the resulting legal pluralism. But there is deeper theoretical significance to three interesting aspects of the Ibaloi case: the first aspect is the obvious role of individual actors in political and economic change; this aspect was explored in Chapter Five. The second aspect is the interesting pattern of interaction between state and local law, and the third is the resulting process of simplification and even ''invention'' of the laws attributed to ''the Other.'' These two aspects will be explored below.

Inventing Cultures: Contrasting Jural Authorities

Communities in Southeast Asia are said to operate under remarkably similar formal, although unwritten, bodies of *adat* law, which are mostly administered by a community council-of-elders.[1] In respect to land tenure, for example, Sonius (1963:28-30) wrote of Indonesia that: ''unlike Roman Law, where the individual element predominates—the interest of the community is centred on the use to which the individual's property is put.'' The ''right of disposal,'' which is the ''superior right in respect to land'' is held by the

---

1   See Burns 1989 for a critique of this view. For a discussion of types of legal systems, see Newman 1983:53.

community, and while an individual has the right to "enjoy" the land, he cannot alienate or pledge it in any way which denies the community's superior claim. This, I believe, is an example of the simplification and "primitivization" of these non-Western property systems.

In the Cordillera, communities were socially and politically independent of each other, although some political co-operation and trade existed between neighbouring villages and regions. This independence was contingent upon a resource base contained within recognized territorial boundaries. The community as a whole co-operated to protect these boundaries (see Barton 1949:137; Prill-Brett 1975, 1985:3; Tapang 1985:30; Worchester 1906:796). Such community-maintained territorial integrity gave the impression that property within ethnic communities was a communal resource, especially since land, water, natural products and minerals were exploitable through birthright or marriage alliance. While it was true that people could not alienate community resources to outsiders, it is important to realize that individuals and small groups monopolized many resources.

In fact, if we examine Ibaloi jural concepts of property rights and compare them to jural concepts common to the West, a surprisingly similar general principle emerges. Sonius (1963:24) writes of this principle: "there is an awareness that land is so vitally important for the survival of all, that the unrestricted power of individuals over it is unacceptable, and yet on the other hand it is the work of the individual which makes the land productive." Sonius argues that all polities (whether a community or a nation state) must arrive at a balance in property relations such that the right of the group to protect productive resources for the common good does not overshadow the right of individuals to benefit from their own labour. He further argues that in some polities the rights of the common group will find fuller expression than the rights of the individual, while in other polities, the reverse will be true (ibid.:24). But we are dealing with shades along a continuum here and not with mutually exclusive categories. Among the Ibaloi, as among Western nations following "Roman law concepts" (ibid.:19), productive decisions over scarce resources have been made by the individual for the most part and not by a communal group.

The Ibaloi viewed land as basically falling into two categories: virgin land which had no claim on it and was therefore open to exploitation by any member of the community, and productive lands which were removed from general access under the principle of *primi occupanis* (as evidenced by improvements). The exclusive right to use and to benefit from improved lands belonged to the individual(s) who first improved it; these rights were acknowledged by the community and protected in indigenous law.

The community retained some rights in productive or improved property, since alienation of land to non-community members was generally forbidden;

by definition such people were enemies. Under indigenous law, the community was a social group, a "right and duty-bearing unit" in Appell's terms, which had jural recognition. Some of the members of this unit resided in the community and some resided away from it; only the former could utilize their rights to unimproved lands. However, all members retained their inherited rights in lands first developed by their ancestors. This is not so unusual since, according to Sonius (ibid.:19), even in the West, liberal or "full" ownership is always restricted by regulations and laws limiting the interests of the owner versus other interests (of other individuals, groups or of the polity in general).

The kin group also retained some rights, since transfers of property were subject to the approval and notarization of the elders. Kin groups enforced rulings that restricted the alienation of family lands to non-members of the descent group. Thus, the rights in community resources were of several types, ranging from those expressed over a very short time and wide space (as with hunting, fishing or gathering natural products) to those expressed over a very long time and to a well-defined space (as with inherited rights to individual rice paddies). The groups associated with these rights were correspondingly wide, the entire community in the former case, and narrow, a single individual in the latter case. This was true of most Cordillera ethnic groups. Drucker (1977:7) argues that among the Bontok, rights in property may be restricted to an individual, to the members of a nuclear family, to the members of a wider kinship unit, to the members of a co-operative unit, or to the entire community (see also Guy 1958:17).

Ethnographers in the Cordillera Central during the American administration documented the complex jural systems of several tribes, including the Ibaloi (Moss 1919), Kalinga (Barton 1949) and Bontok (Jenks 1905) and did not hesitate to label this phenomenon as "law." In 1929, Governor Early went so far as to argue that these ethnic jural codes should be respected and, where applicable, be recognized in the state court system (Fry 1983:137). However, the gold boom in the 1930s resulted in legislation against native mining and panning operations in Benguet (Tapang 1985:31), and other "benevolent" legislation undercut native land tenure, slavery and usury (Keesing and Keesing 1934:166-70). The American administration subsequently declined to take Governor Early's advice. In Benguet, as in other colonial areas of the world, indigenous law was dismissed as barbaric, static, reactionary and not conducive to rapid social, economic and political "progress," despite the ethnographic data that provided evidence for the changing, adaptive nature of indigenous law.

For example, Moss (1919:237) observed communitywide meetings in Ibaloi villages where new laws were formulated or old ones were given new sanctions. The Ibaloi term for law is *din'teg*, which literally means "to make straight'' (Scheerer 1905:170). The linguistic suggestion is of an ongoing process, not a static achievement. Community consensus was required before any change would be ratified by the elders, or the *ma'ngi'din'teg*, meaning: ''the ones who will make things straight.'' The meetings to decide on changes were called *olnong* —as opposed to the normal dispute-resolution meetings, or tong tong.

The Spanish and American administrations could gain little benefit from a colony, however, without first extinguishing native claims to resources. The Spanish administration promulgated the Regalian Doctrine, replacing the sovereignty of native peoples with that of the Spanish crown (Aranal-Sereno and Libarios 1983). They then demanded tribute or taxation to help finance the religious, judicial and political administration which justified the Regalian Doctrine. Under the later American administration, Moss (1919:237) notes that the judicial proceedings in Ibaloi villages were placed under the authority of a few influential men, presumably because they understood the desired American changes. This important step in political incorporation attenuated the indigenous jural process. Thus, Spain and the United States, like other European colonial powers, extinguished the primary or territorial right of political sovereignty of indigenous peoples, which in turn supports the secondary or usufruct right of individuals in property. In order to do this, Westerners ''invented'' a customary law which had all the opposite characteristics of those desired in progressive nation states. This categorization of non-Western law and of the ''alien other'' allowed Europeans to sharpen their self-definition; the resulting two-way process of the cultural ''invention'' has had continuing ramifications (see Wolf 1982). However, while Westerners argued that indigenous law was different for reasons of their own, we cannot ignore the possibility that a similarly stark contrast between indigenous and state law has also been invented by *local* participants for reasons of *their* own, and then later absorbed by ethnographers as empirical reality.

No society has ever lived in pristine isolation; there has always been the need to respond to changes in political, economic and jural environments. Among the Ibaloi, local normative orders and cultural systems have taken their present form as a result of long-term, complex processes involving local people and all sorts of outside contacts. As the state improved its ability to politically incorporate isolated regions, multiple jural codes were promulgated in Ibaloi villages. Some were based on past practice and some were drawn from Western jural concepts imposed by the state; still others were based on a synthesis or on a simplified contrast between the two. Consequently, individuals involved in disputes over the status of people or things had an extremely complex and flexible grab-bag of jural concepts to draw on.

But is there any real difference between indigenous and state jural systems? In Chapter Six, for example, it was evident that both local and state adjudicators sometimes suggest similar solutions to disputes.

Kladze (1983:75) argues that indigenous law and state law *have* significant differences. Indigenous law finds authority in "custom" (in the Ibaloi case, by traditional practice followed and sanctioned by the ancestors), and emphasizes reconciliation and flexibility (see also Benda-Beckmann 1979:117,138). Each case is unique, since the flexible codes of indigenous law allow a solution to be sought that satisfies all concerned. Restitution to the wronged party is considered more important than punishment of the offender. In contrast, state law is said to be clear-cut and predictable, operating as it does on the procedures of evidence and precedence, both of which ignore consensus and continued social harmony as end goals (Benda-Beckmann 1979:138). Kladze (1983:75) argues that these supposed attributes of state law may be the attraction for some litigants. These are certainly the aspects of state law which Ibaloi elders identify and condemn. They tell disputants that the confrontational approach to conflict resolution generates one winner and one loser and that litigants come away from a court case as "enemies, unable to act amicably together in the future." This predictable rule-determined outcome in state courts is contrasted with the flexibility and understanding of the elders' mediation. Further, the elders point out that decisions rendered in state courts are often ignored in the social arenas of local communities.

In Moss (1919), however, we find evidence for an indigenous interest in determining the guilty party, including guilt by ordeal (ibid.:267-69), as well as varieties of corporal punishment for offenders (ibid.:263). Further, according to older people we spoke to, law before political incorporation was not always fair, impartial or universal. Baknang were said to order poor men hung by the heels merely for taking fruit from their trees. Children of the poor were whipped for similar crimes. Where is the "amicable settlement" in such scenarios? It would appear that where litigants were social equals, mediation prevailed. Where litigants were not equals, adjudication by a council drawn from members of elite families was more likely, with a predictable outcome in favour of the social superior.

While Americans were not the first Europeans to influence Ibaloi culture, changes introduced by their administration of the uplands included first, the strengthening of elite powers through bureaucratic appointments, and subsequently, the removal of the judicial process out of village hands (see also Kladze 1983:76). I argue that it was only after political incorporation had reached this point that customary law began to take its present form. The few sanctions remaining to Kabayan elders included scolding, public condemnation of certain actions, fines in the form of food or alcohol for council members or as restitution for damages and, of course, ostracism and loss of economic or emotional support. The amicable settlement took on more significance in this context.

The amicable settlement remains elusive in cases where one of the litigants is non-Ibaloi or where an Ibaloi is not susceptible to methods of peer pressure such as losing the respect of related elders who are potential landlords or who may deny an inheritance. And increasingly within Ibaloi society, there is a lack of consensus over the nature of "customary law." Consequently, the elders' remaining methods of enforcement are further weakened by a resulting lack of compliance. Local people seem equally adept at ignoring elders' rulings and state court decisions; this is another thing that state and local law have in common.

Nevertheless, the people of Kabayan do distinguish between customary and state law, and the elders refer to this distinction at every turn in order to shore up their own decisions. At one tong tong I attended, a man became angry when denied a divorce. He was told by the elders to "go get one from the government," an obvious reference to the difficulty of doing so in a Catholic society. When people were intransigent over elders-mediated inheritance divisions, they were reminded that the state rules that all must inherit equally. Everyone knows that land fractionalization is bad enough as it is. The elders, community officials and barangay courts will draw on accepted indigenous rules in reaching a decision but are equally capable of evolving new approaches through contrast with the state normative order. For this reason, I hold that at least two clear levels of jural authority are part of the operation of dispute resolution among local people in Kabayan, whether or not they have accurate information on the content of the legal codes of "the Other." The question is, how have these contrasting jural codes been useful to people?

Who Benefits? Social Stratification and Unforeseen Consequences

Given the influence of legal instrumentalist theory (see Collins 1982, Hunt 1985, Stone 1985, Wells 1987), it is often assumed that one effect of legal pluralism is more alternatives for the wealthy and fewer for the poor in terms of access to dispute resolution. That is to say, the poor would be forced to rely on the decisions of the local system, even when they know they would benefit from a state court decision, since they cannot afford legal fees and protracted delays. In contrast, wealthier litigants (especially if they reside outside of the community), may force an appeal of a local decision, knowing that a state court decision may go in their favour, or that judges can be "influenced." But the relationship between social stratification and jural processes, whether at the local or at the state level, is a subject for empirical investigation. Interestingly enough, in Kabayan, a far more complex pattern of dispute-resolution venue and personal strategies is indicated; one that supports a re-thinking of simplistic notions of the relationship between wealth, political power and jural process.

While the wealthy were once able to monopolize community resources and to pass them on as inherited properties, subsequent events have whittled away at the value or size of these holdings. Today, few of the formerly affluent families have been able to maintain control over land in the face of encroachment sanctioned by state law and of fragmentation through inheritance. It is interesting, for example, to compare the current landholdings for three upwardly mobile households of abiteg background shown in Table 5 with the progressive deterioration of the household landholdings in three generations of a baknang family shown in Table 6.

TABLE 5
Landholdings in Hectares by Land-type among Upwardly Mobile Households of Abiteg Background

Household Number	Rice	Camote Fruit	Pasture	Totals
125	.4670	15.7600	nil	16.2270
103	1.5634	5.0006	nil	6.5640
155	.5169	8.8286	nil	9.3455
Total	2.5473	29.5892	nil	32.1365

Households of abiteg background such as those in Table 5 have acquired irrigated landholdings which are larger than those of many households of baknang descent. Camote/fruit lands show the largest increase in size of holdings among abiteg households. Some of these holdings have been acquired since World War II under the new state land tenure regulations and some have been acquired through purchase. Income from wage labour in the mining industry, transport and bureaucracy have been used to acquire land. On the other hand, many descendants of baknang in the community have not managed to hang onto the holdings their ancestors acquired. Although the elite such as Kamista were the innovators in introducing new property-right principles, this strategy has not always served their children and grandchildren to the same advantage.

Table 6 demonstrates that in one family of baknang descent, each successive generation after the apical male (estimated life span 1844-1936) saw their holdings decline in their children's generation. This is related to inheritance patterns as well as to fragmentation. Although the eldest son of the apical ancestor inherited more than his two siblings, he in turn had nine children. Five of these children inherited land; three of the five were spinster daughters who remained in the family home, limiting fragmentation for their generation. However, their land is now worked by a number of nieces and nephews who will inherit. Table 6 graphically shows that the advantages accruing to a family because of socio-economic status in one generation did not necessarily prevail for all members in the next. But neither inheritance patterns nor fragmentation explain the noticeable deterioration of the total family holdings between generations II and III. This deterioration holds true for all land-types except pasture: rice land has declined by 1.5408 hectares, or 30 percent of the original holdings and camote lands have declined by 5.4480 hectares, or 16 percent of the original holdings.

TABLE 6
Landholdings in Hectares by Land-type through Three Generations of Households Descended from a Single Baknang

Generation	Descent Line	Rice	Camote	Pasture	Totals
I	Apical male (3 children)	n/a	n/a	n/a	n/a*
II	A. Eldest son (9 children)	2.3799	20.7169	45.8089	68.9057
	B. Daughter (3 children)	1.7478	12.4604	34.0000	48.2082
	C. Son (2 children)	.8563	.0944	nil	.9507
Subtotal Generation II		4.9840	33.2717	79.8089	118.0646
III	A1. 3 spinsters	.1453	.7046	26.8089	27.6588
	A2. Eldest son (2 children)	.7304	.3662	19.0000	20.0966
	A3. Son (1 child)	nil	16.5000	nil	16.5000
Subtotal Descent Line A		.8757	17.5708	45.8089	64.2554
	B1. Eldest son (5 children)	.7304	7.0000	20.0000	28.2500
	B2. Daughter (3 children)	.0233	3.1105	14.0000	17.1335
Subtotal Descent Line B		1.2733	10.1105	34.0000	45.3845
	C1. Eldest Son (8 children)	.5959	.0524	nil	.6483
	C2. Daughter	.6983	.0900	nil	.7883
Subtotal Descent Line C		1.2942	.1424	nil	1.4366
Total Generation III		3.4432	27.8237	79.8089	111.0765

* All holdings are based on tax records and self-declaration of unregistered lands. Holdings for the apical male ancestor can be estimated by those of his offspring, since each of these claim to have inherited their holdings from their father. Note that elder children tend to inherit more and that some children inherit no land.

The decline in landholdings demonstrated in Table 6 is one of the unintended consequences of the introduction of external normative concepts of tenure, and of the interaction of local and state concepts. In this family, some rice lands were lost when landslides resulted from mining operations made possible by discrepancies between state and local tenure regulations. Camote/fruit landholdings were encroached on under the tax-declaration tenure regulations, and the productivity of rice paddies declined as a result of irrigation water theft.

This evidence demonstrates that Kladze (1983:77) offers too simplistic a solution when he writes: "It is submitted that the sole criterion for the validity of a rule of customary law must be the demonstrated or demonstrable acceptance or assent of the community or ethnic group in which it is applicable." This presumes a degree of homogeneity or of common interests within communities for which there is little evidence in most human societies. For certain people in Kabayan, the advantages of two contrasting legal orders have been greater than those of a single legal system. These people have not necessarily formed a particular class or division of society, but rather, are those who utilized a common strategy in the competition over resources. Some of these people may have been aware of common interests, but the major influence has been the tendency to mimic the successful strategies of innovators. Here the state/local differences in legal codes are less significant than the existence of alternative codes and the patterns of their application. In the Ibaloi context, it appears that if state law had not existed, someone would have had to invent it, and in a real sense, they did. I am reminded here of Goody's (1983) recent work on the transformation of European kin systems under the influence of the bureaucratization of the Christian church. In that case, religious routinization was the source for competitive normative orders in human society. The ultimate source of alternative rules may be less important than the way in which they are utilized in ongoing individual strategies. Such strategies are tied to competition over resources. The sources and consequences of the rise of such purposive strategies and their use in resource competition will become more apparent in the following discussion of economic transformations.

Part Two: Economic Transformations in Ibaloi History

Alternative jural authorities and social stratification within Kabayan increased the conflict over productive resources. Where parties did not receive adequate support for their claims from one jural order, they could always appeal to the other. Conflicting interests are one reason that Ibaloi communities did not remain closed to external pressures in the way that neighbouring Bontok, and until recently, Kalinga villages did. Several questions are raised by contrasting these ethnic groups: for example, how did conflicting interests develop in Ibaloi society and what is the nature of the ties between those having such interests? Did those with similar interests form groups, and if so what was the criteria for recruitment to them and how were they organized? Finally, what sorts of property were they concerned with and how did they change? This contrast and the resulting questions are addressed below.

The Ibaloi Difference: Cross-Cultural Evidence from the Cordillera

There are similarities in the way property is held and transferred in most Cordilleran ethnic groups. Individuals can open new swidden lands, cultivate woodlots, establish fishing sites and build irrigated rice terraces on virgin community lands. For most Cordilleran ethnic groups, rules differ for inherited property (developed by former generations), conjugal property (developed by a married couple in the present generation), moveable property, real estate and other resources, depending on economic value and degree of improvements. In Bontok communities, when a young couple marry, they each are awarded some inherited property from their individual families (Keesing 1949:586). The parents evaluate the economic capabilities of the new couple to judge whether lands will finally be devolved to them. Similar practices exist among the Ibaloi, Kankanaey, Ifugao and Kalinga. The inherited lands of one spouse never pass over into the hands of the family of the other in any of these groups (see Botengan 1976:80). None of them require that the property of an individual or nuclear family revert back to the communal holdings with death or changing circumstances in the family development cycle (for comparison see Behar 1984). The degree of individual control over property is variable and appears to be affected by the strength of the cognatic descent group[2] or of the village ward. The present-day Ibaloi, however, have the fewest restrictions on individual control of property of any of the comparable Cordilleran ethnic groups. To understand the reasons for this it is necessary to briefly contrast the property relations of some of these groups with the Ibaloi.

The sharpest contrast is provided by the Bontok. In this society, group rights in property are important, a fact visible in devolution regulations. The eldest child receives the largest amount of conjugal as well as inherited rice fields. However, the eldest girl must receive some inherited lands from her

---

2   According to Eggan (1967:188) the term cognatic descent group was first coined by Firth (1963) to refer to all the descendants of a single couple traced through both the male and female line.

mother (thus maintaining a link with the mother's cognatic descent group) while the oldest boy similarly inherits from his father (Prill-Brett 1975:12-13). Younger siblings may inherit conjugal rice paddies as individuals, and all children will inherit conjugal swidden lands, pasture, fishing sites, woodlots and irrigation systems to be held jointly (Botengan 1976:69,75,83). As generations pass, the wealth of senior children (also called kadangyan among the Bontok) is ensured (Keesing 1949:594). On the other hand, common holdings of the cognatic descent groups are also ensured, although these may be sold, and developed into rice paddies to start the cycle over again, or held by a wider and wider group until they take on an open-access aspect. Both Drucker (1977:7) and Prill-Brett (ibid.) note this cyclical pattern to property relations in Bontok communities. Eggan (1967:198) argues that other Cordilleran ethnic groups have so-called "corporate" bilateral descent groups (i.e., property-holding units), including the Ifugao (ibid.:188,191) and the Kankanaey speakers of Sagada (ibid.:197). Few have the complicated inheritance laws of the Bontok. The Ifugao, for example, devolve the majority of inherited property to a single heir (Barton 1969:43-45).

Earlier analysts saw the erosion of kinship ties as a necessary first step towards a more modern political organization. Eggan (1967:198-99, 1963: 352) argues that the territorial-based unit or ward has advantages over kinship units and becomes more common with increased population pressure and the territorial stability imposed by wet-rice agriculture. He feels that the ward was spreading among Cordilleran groups at the time of American contact. The Bontok are cited as the best example, with their *ator*—which is defined as a neighbourhood group cross-cut by patrilineal ties (see also Keesing 1949:579,587 and Jenks 1905:49-50). Prill-Brett (1985:11) re-examines the Bontok ator and shows it to be an association of male representatives of families which together own property such as swiddens, forest stands, rice fields, real estate or fishing sites. These resources are exploited by any member of the group, and in addition, may be sold or used to finance ator activities such as ritual events connected with headhunting, feuding, and peace pacts (see also Drucker 1977:8). However, the membership of a single ator is not drawn from a common residence area within the village, and while affiliation is usually through the male line, there are means whereby membership can be by choice. Since ator ties cross-cut and supplement corporate kin group (or tayan) ties, Eggan's argument is questionable.

One interesting aspect of the atar is that the eldest members serve as the Bontok judiciary (Jenks 1905:32), responsible for judging their own ator members. A council of such elders drawn from all ator within the village forms the *intugtukan* (Richards 1950:89), the supreme judicial and political authority for the community. As with the corporate kin-based tayan, the ator holds collective responsibility for the actions of its individual members (see Bacdayan 1980:175). This indicates little conflict between the role of the ator and the role of the tayan in Bontok communities. The former includes the latter in its operation as a supra-kin-group organization without superseding the economic, political or social role of the kinship group. Multiple levels of group-based property rights are not necessarily in conflict, nor is the attenuation of one necessary for the benefit of the other.

While craft specialization such as salt production, pottery, mining and smelting has been controlled by kin groups in some Cordilleran villages (see Jenks 1905:118,146), the most common kin-group property rights are found in land (Moss 1919:249, Barton 1949:51). For example, sale of inherited land is usually restricted to members of the bilateral descent group or requires their permission (see Barton 1949:107-109, 1969:32; Bello 1972:156; Botengan 1976:12-13; Eggan 1967:197; Guy 1958:18; Moss 1919:249). Further, kin-group rights are widely used in the Cordillera to establish access to land (Drucker 1977:15) despite the fact that more people are experiencing Western-style education and employment in the cash economy. While the old ways are increasingly coming under attack, the Ibaloi pattern is not yet prevalent. State land title is breaking down the corporate holdings of tayan and ator in some Bontok communities (Botengan 1976:85) and such titles are sometimes used by a few to the disadvantage of the majority (see Lawless 1978: 145,153 and Bello 1972:83), but many Bontok see advantages in traditional practice. This widespread viewpoint is probably one reason for general Cordilleran resistance to state land-title programs.

Ibaloi land-tenure rules and kinship organization indicate that they too had corporate kinship units (the bunak) holding property together and sharing responsibility for the actions of members of the group. But forces acting on the bunak caused their decline in Ibaloi society a full century before such kin groups came under attack in other Cordilleran ethnic groups. The post-Spanish developments connected with the gold trade meant that the resources and strengths of the bunak became less important (and perhaps even liabilities) at the same time that new alliances built on wealth and mutual interests were emerging. The impact of these new alliances is suggested by similar events in other areas of the world, where new economic interests for one strata of society have required that property interests be wrenched out of the hands of groups and placed in the hands of individuals. Lam (1983), for example, found that the Hawaiian nobility gained individual tenure in lands only by denying the rights of various indigenous ''corporate'' groups. The Hawaiian royal family subsequently found themselves faced with the more powerful corporate groups of the colonial society, to whom they lost control of the land. A very similar process developed in the Ibaloi case.

The Rise of Social Stratification

Scott (1974:48) shows that historic descriptions of the Cordillera Central Igorot differ little from earlier accounts of pre-Spanish lowland Filipino culture. The entire Philippines shared culture traits developing out of independent communities, led in their economic pursuits and in internecine war by an upper strata headed by a chief, or *datu*. For lowland Filipinos, achieved positions of military valour became ascribed administrative positions under the process of political incorporation into the Spanish colonial empire. Among the Ibaloi, the transition from an indigenous achievement-based hierarchy to ascribed status proceeded without direct Spanish involvement. The question is, why?

The Keesings (1934:57,161) argue that the powerful kadangyan families in Ibaloi society were directly associated with irrigated rice culture and that ''a keen sense of individual ownership of natural resources'' flourished in regions with irrigation. Eggan (1963:252-55) discusses a similar change in southern Kalinga villages after the adoption of wet-rice technology (see also Lawless 1978). However, the Keesings (1934:189) also point out that, historically, the majority of Ibaloi people practised shifting horticulture (see also Keesing 1962:65 and Barnett 1967). Why would a society which adopted irrigated rice cultivation later and less fully than surrounding groups be more strongly affected by the correlation of irrigation with social stratification?

Spanish expeditions into the Cordillera Central in the sixteenth century documented an ''aristocracy'' among the gold-trading Igorots (see Blair and Robertson 1973,vol. 20:270, Scott 1974:199), although wet rice was not documented until the eighteenth century (Scott 1974:149,177). By the latter period, the Ibaloi lived in several different types of communities. Wet-rice towns were as large as 600 houses (ibid.:174) while mining settlements were small, with scattered housing, suggesting a less cohesive social structure. Swidden communities and gold-trade centres had yet a different appearance. Each type of community had a different resource base, social organization and political structure. In which of these communities did ascribed social status and a closed hierarchy emerge?

Swidden communities predate the other forms. In the earliest Spanish records the mountain slopes in the Benguet area were said to be denuded of all but a few scattered pine trees (Blair and Robertson 1973,vol. 20:268), suggesting swidden activity. Houses were scattered among the fields or along the mountain peaks for defence. The leaders were ''the head of their kinfolk'' which comprised only 10 to 12 households (ibid.:270). Leaders were renowned head-takers, feared by their neighbours, but it is doubtful that their influence extended beyond their family circle. Gold-mining communities appear next in the historical record and were described as individually held gold tunnels exploited by families and their retainers, all of whom lived in homes at the mouth of the tunnels. Individual ownership was common, extending to the tunnels as well as to the slaves who worked them. Chiefly leaders existed in these communities (Scott 1974:151); but it is not clear if their leadership depended on wealth and prestige as the most successful gold producer or if they were able to exert an influence beyond their kin network or community (ibid.:220).

Another type of community relying on gold was found along strategic mountain passes and trails, the better to control the flow of trade to the low-lands. Ibaloi folk history places the rise of ascribed status in these communi-ties, where the descendants of Amkidit created a dynasty of gold traders. Trade towns were large and had the most contact with the Spanish. They framed early Spanish perceptions of the Benguet Igorot as so rich in gold that they did not have to grow their own food (Blair and Robertson 1973, vol. 14:383). The success of these trade centres relied on astute political alli-ances with neighbouring Ibaloi gold-producing villages, peace pacts with oth-ers, and intermarriage into still others and into lowlands trade communities (see Scott 1974:117). Leaders were wealthy even by European standards, with large political followings resembling military cadres (ibid.:187). These followers were supported with the profits of the gold trade and were used to police traffic with the lowlands (ibid.:184). The amount of silver money, as well as gold currency circulating in such towns surprised the priests of the Tonglo mission, who also documented usury, debt peonage and slavery (ibid.:115-20).

Finally, a fourth type of Ibaloi community was found in suitable, well-watered areas of the upper reaches of the Agno River valley. These riverine settlements combined elements of all the proceeding types of communities; they grew wet rice in irrigated paddies to supplement dryland production of root crops, produced gold ore (Scott 1974:184), slave raided to the north, entered into peace pacts and intermarried with Amkidit's gold-intermediary family (ibid.:118). Wet-rice towns were often pioneered by gold traders seek-ing both pasture for their herds of livestock and economic diversification (see Bagamaspad and Hamada-Pawid 1985). They developed after the arrival of the Spanish, the subsequent restriction of the gold trade and rise of the gold-trading elite.

By the mid-nineteenth century these four types of communities co-existed, creating some ethnographic confusion for visitors to the region. The role of property and the development of social stratification differed slightly between them, especially in the degree to which the upper strata came to have an economic monopoly in the productive resources of the com-munity. Are the folk explanations reliable? Did ascribed status emerge in the gold-trade communities and spread from there as gold traders diversified their economic pursuits? In theory the connection between trade and stratification is an old one, and this explanation is used by many Cordilleran scholars (Guy 1958:62, Scott 1974:184 and Tapang 1985). However, trade alone is not sufficient cause for the development of ascribed positions of power and prestige. I have examined this process in some detail elsewhere (see Wiber 1989) and will only briefly discuss it here to demonstrate its importance to the rise of ascribed position and cultural heterogeneity.

Lawless (1978:147) argues that in the context of an environment such as the Cordillera Central, when a people trade across contrasting environmental regions, wealth tends to be created through "price-difference trading." Resources which make trade possible are available to all residents of a community. Wealth generated by an individual through exchange is allocated among community members in a redistributive fashion (Sahlins 1958, Strathern 1971). However, if impinging forces disrupt the flow of this trade, the wealth-generating context changes (Lawless 1978:147). When traders can no longer freely trade outside their community or region, they often engage in price-difference trading within it, through a monopolization of productive resources. Wealth can then support ascribed positions of power and prestige. Lawless shows that in Kalinga society, usury, manipulation of societal norms and monopolizing scarce resources followed from a disruption in normal trade relations which took place in the early twentieth century. Rigid social stratification developed, and "trading up" was no longer possible (ibid.:147). A similar pattern developed in Ibaloi society as early as the seventeenth century.

Benguet area natives traded gold for Chinese pottery, trade beads, cloth, iron and animals well before the arrival of the Spanish. Folk tales suggest that gold was treated as an open-access resource in those days. One story tells of how: "It was easy to fill sacks with gold and the metal was in abundance for everyone" (Bagamaspad and Hamada-Pawid 1985:68). Power and prestige depended not only on wealth redistribution and military valour in the endemic, interregional headhunting and feuding (ibid.:220), but also on the successful establishment of trade contacts (Blair and Robertson 1973, vol. 20: 270 and Scott 1974:187). A leader stood between two social universes, maintaining reliable trade contacts in the lowlands and a following in the community. Leaders and their followers were interdependent, and social mobility depended on skill in interpersonal relationships. However, the Spanish interference in one social universe rapidly began to create changes in the other after the late sixteenth century.

Scott (1974:14) argues that the first response to Spanish military forays was to curtail gold-mining activities to "present a less attractive target."

Between 1571, when Salcedo first entered the Cordillera Central, and Quirante's expedition of 1624, the amount of gold entering the lowlands was so minimal that Quirante openly doubted the existence of the fabled Igorot mines. This Ibaloi ruse was so well carried out that the Spanish never developed commercial gold mines in Benguet, although in the eighteenth century they did open copper mines (Scott 1974:246). But what did the success of this ruse mean for people who had formerly relied on the gold trade? The above-mentioned folk-tale suggests the answer; it continues: "After years of amassing wealth, man became lazy, proud, cruel, unruly and uncharitable. A wide gap formed between the few rich and the countless poor" (ibid.:68). The Ibaloi culture hero Amkidit was one such rich man.

His response to the new situation was to organize a controlling network of family members and allies on the western slopes of the Cordillera Central and to regulate the amount and beneficiaries of the gold still being traded. To do this, he and his allies had to limit contact between gold producers and gold buyers, creating an intermediary position for themselves. From this point on, the evidence for an increasingly rigid stratification can be found. Henceforth, the "principalia" of the Ibaloi areas acted out of a concern to protect a favoured position in Ibaloi society. The fierce resistance against Spanish intrusions (which continued in other areas of the Cordillera) was abandoned by the Ibaloi, and first missions and later military commands were tolerated in Ibaloi territory. First gold, then tobacco, and finally cattle, coffee and rice paddies followed each other as the elite stock-in-trade. The peshit feasts became the prerogative of those families who inherited the right to perform them. Headhunting and raiding into the lowlands was repressed as inimical to the elite interests (Scott 1974:291). Prestige formerly obtained through such military pursuits became unimportant as an avenue to political power.

Amkidit's followers soon monopolized most productive resources by the simple expediency of controlling the labour which made them productive. The restricted gold trade made it possible to gain a monopoly over cattle and meat, both as commodities and as ritualized gifts in the florescent ancestor-worship rituals (see Wiber 1989). Both served to attract labourers to the gold traders; large-scale construction projects such as irrigation canals or paddy walls were accomplished by exchanging meat for labour. More skilled labour was recompensed with live animals; people claim that many Kabayan terrace systems were constructed by Ifugao workers in this way. The encatlo, or "share" system of the cowhand, who earned "one leg" of each animal born in the herd under his care (Tapang 1985:11-13), was also an exchange of labour for animals. Ibaloi customary law developed in ways that expanded and reinforced this control of labour. For example, a breech of law was punished by fines or indemnity, usually in the form of an animal sacrifice and feast for the elders of the community. If the accused could not pay, then debt slavery resulted (Scott 1974:188). The religious belief system played a role in this process, since the "cañao imperative" could also result in debt slavery. Control of labour was soon translated into the control of other productive resources such as irrigated land, pasture and swidden. Internal usury, debt slavery and the manipulation of societal customs developed a stratified system which was extreme for the Cordillera Central.

Furthermore, until the mid-twentieth century, the elite maintained their privileged position through every new economic and political development. Even taxation initially worked to their advantage; independent swiddeners could only pay their taxes by coming down into the valleys to work for the "well-to-do owners of terraces" (Scott 1974:291). The introduction of bureaucratic changes such as property registration and land titles benefitted the elite, although since the indigenous basis for control over real estate is not entirely clear, it is difficult to estimate the significance of this. For example, under indigenous tenure practice, how did the elite gain control over pasture lands? Tapang (1985:14 and 28) argues that early in the nineteenth century, when the elite began to breed cattle rather than importing them from the lowlands, access to pasture was based on indigenous tenure. This may be true, but appropriation by the few at the expense of the rights of the many seems a more likely scenario.

There are ethnographic precedents for this interpretation. Indigenous land tenure among the Vanuatu did not prevent the development of new forms of social inequality when economic conditions changed (Rodman 1984). As with the Ibaloi, indigenous land-tenure laws were flexible and allowed for "the practice of land acquisition by encroachment," usually by the politically and economically powerful against weaker members of their own kin group (ibid.:65). It is known that the Ibaloi elite entrusted herds to relatives or clients who had bunak-based or community-membership-based rights in lands suitable for pasture. In subsequent years, the peculiarities of state tenure legislation made the owner of the herds the owner of the pastures as well. Funeral rites allowed for competition over inherited lands; those who paid for funeral offerings got the land. These people were often collateral relatives who inherited at the expense of the deceased's offspring (ibid.:68). Maine (1901:192) compares Roman and "Hindoo" inheritance law and finds similar devolution practices. Residual property rights held by the descent group play a vital role in such "acquisition by encroachment."

The success of this ploy can be estimated from the result of early American administration attempts to redistribute lands to the poor in Benguet. The wealthy in each region could establish some kind of claim to any productive lands (Keesing and Keesing 1934:166). Descent-group membership, marriage ties and use were utilized to establish rights which then justified acquisition of state title. As in Vanuatu society, this encroachment was initially tolerated by local people because in the past, rights would always be remembered and asserted after the death of the usurper (Rodman 1984:65). However, neither the Vanuatu nor the Ibaloi foresaw that usurpers could freeze the recycling of land among the descent-group membership by first improving the productive capacity of the land (coffee plantations, rice terraces, gold mines) and second, by acquiring state title.

Some people argue that social stratification is widespread and persistent because it has some advantages (Keesing and Keesing 1934:198, Lynch 1979). Ibaloi folk history agrees with this perspective to a point. The kadangyan were organizers and innovators in agricultural development. Tied into reciprocal relationships with their retainers, they were viewed as benefactors and culture heros (see Bagamaspad and Hamada-Pawid 1985:49-62). They found gold sites, mined the ore, traded for cattle, created a livestock industry, developed irrigation and wet-rice paddy systems, and attracted dependents whom they supported and employed. One elder told me that when you belonged to a kadangyan household, every little detail of your life was taken care of, right down to the animals to be butchered for your wedding or funeral. But people also say that over time the kadangyan were able to shed many of their traditional responsibilities at the same time that they consolidated their hold on wealth and privilege.

The Ibaloi and other upland groups do not differ in the existence of social stratification, but rather in the degree of differentiation between elite and commoner. In other Cordilleran societies the elite members could not translate wealth and respect into power and the usurping of productive resources. The system of Ibaloi stratification was able to develop for several reasons. First, internalization of trade relations transformed kin and neighbours into economic resources; an example is the introduction of usury, which remains forbidden in Bontok society. Second, headhunting and internecine war had created ties which cut across status boundaries, making people interdependent for defence. The strategies of the Ibaloi elite ended these security threats. Corporate property-holding groups such as the bunak, which distributed the rights in productive resources over a large group, were attacked at their foundation when their jural control over an estate was challenged. While bunak ties were often useful in establishing land rights for state title, the descent groups declined as private rights were strengthened with state title. Finally, the development of the baknang, or chief, created an ascribed position to which only those with birthright could aspire. The Ibaloi themselves attribute these changes in their culture to the actions of individual innovators such as

Amkidit and his descendants. Support for this interpretation is found in more recent culture history, as well.

Part Three: Individual Strategies and the Rise of Communalism

The view of the Cordilleran village as "communal" is widespread. For example, Aranal-Sereno and Libarios (1983:438) write:

> Not only is land viewed as communal; even production is communal. To be able to cultivate and produce enough rice in the hilly slopes requires constant, efficient work on a scale impossible for an individual to achieve. Without communal organization, it is difficult, if not impossible, to sustain a self-sufficient and subsistent Kalinga community.

This mis-perception is common not only to outside observers but to many educated Igorots, as well:

> It is a common observation among lawyers of [Benguet] Province that in many instances it is the predominant practice of our people in the past to have a land title be named to a single individual, although the parcel of land embraced and covered by the said title is owned, and possessed by several individuals and/or families of the community. Understandably, this practice was devised for convenience purposes and to curb extra expenses as well. In addition, it is my personal observation that our people are proned [*sic*] and inclined to this set-up because of our communal oriented culture (Bacoling 1984:9-10).

The author of this passage argues that block titles resulted from communal tendencies in Igorot communities. While in his case, the use of the term communal may result from semantic confusion, similar descriptions of indigenous Cordilleran tenure practices are frequently found in more scholarly publications (as shown above), as well as in bureaucratic publications (see, for example, de los Reyes 1980, de los Reyes et al. 1980). Here the term communal is used as a form of shorthand to describe many different kinds of group tenure in resources resulting in the widespread misinterpretation of native tenure. This mis-perception is now affecting the operation of property systems because it has affected the individual purposive strategies being pursued in communities such as Kabayan (see Chapter Five).

As I have indicated, the problem seems to arise from two factors; first, a misunderstanding of the property rights found in indigenous communities, and second, the misuse of the term "communal" to cover all cases of interest being held by more than one individual in any scarce good. The first factor is as common as the second. Dove (1982:15), for example, writes: "One misconception, with far-reaching consequences, pertains to the 'communal' nature of peasant or tribal life." He found that Indonesian officials tried to repress the Dayak longhouse because of its "communal" organization, which was associated with communism and was viewed as inimical to progress founded on the individualistic economic development of nuclear family hold-ings (ibid.:18-19). On the other hand, Western development personnel sought to employ the reputed communal organization of the longhouse as an asset in development projects. These development plans were unsuccessful, as the programs were built upon a fundamental misconception of Dayak property relations (ibid.:21).

Dove (ibid.:25) and Appell (1974:8) argue that the Dayak and Rungus longhouse is actually a collection of discrete, independently owned family compartments. Further, while an important shared resource of all longhouse members is "the right to all land in the longhouse territory," in fact,

> the territorial rights of the longhouse are residual rights. Primary rights, meaning rights of use and of devolution (by gift, exchange, sale or inheri-tance) are held either by individual households or by small clusters of households related through partition (Dove 1982:32).

Dove recognizes the important difference between territorial rights in the land held by the group in common, and usufruct rights in the land as held by indi-viduals or groups of individuals. Van Vollenhoven called the former the "right of allocation" and the latter "preferential rights" (see Burns 1989: 51-52). This is a basic distinction, which when unobserved creates confusion and the misapplication of the communal concept.

Recognizing the four historic types of Ibaloi village extant at the time of American contact makes it easy to see why early administrators drew the conclusions that the Ibaloi were changed by contact with the Spanish. In comparison with other Cordilleran ethnic groups with a single, territorially closed community type, the swidden villages of the Ibaloi appeared to be the indigenous form. Other types of Ibaloi villages were perceived as having a culturally contaminated social organization stimulated by the Spanish (see Keesing and Keesing 1934:68,74; Keesing 1962:64; *Report of the Philippine Commission 1900*, vol. 1:45, Richards 1950:61). The fact that the Ibaloi bak-nang had social status, wealth and political power to a degree not found in other ethnic groups indicated to American administrators that the communal rights and economic independence of the poorer strata had been eroded by the Spanish colonial administration. Thus the early American administration in Benguet attempted to redress the situation. Ironically, this same American administration upheld the Regalian Doctrine and introduced the Torrens land title system (see Aranal-Sereno and Libarios 1983).

This approach, in addition to the American policy of promoting individ-ual tenure, undercut efforts to improve the lot of the poor in Benguet. Under this administration, group rights in land which provided insurance for poorer members of the community were defenceless against appropriation by the wealthy or well-informed. Attempts to promote individual holdings resulted in the consolidation of land into a few hands (see Afrika Instituut Leiden 1951:118, Bastin 1954:92, Feeny 1977:12, Lyon 1970:11, Money 1861:69, Tomosugi 1980:14 for similar results in other contexts). The economic position of the kadangyan families of Benguet came under attack at the beginning of the American administration. They lost control over labour for several reasons: new religious beliefs were introduced, making it less likely that people would become debt slaves to obtain animals for cañao; new laws prevented slavery and debt peonage; alternative forms of employment in the cash economy drew retainers away; and universal education created new expectations among the poor. The elite responded by consolidating their hold on the land, using the state-promoted individual title. This consolidation was not seriously challenged in most Ibaloi communities until the aftermath of World War II.

World War II was a watershed in the history of the Philippines and of Benguet (see Fry 1983:218, Leano 1958:7-8 and Tapang 1985:5). It began the final decline of the Ibaloi elite. The Japanese occupation destroyed elite cattle herds, already reduced by competition over grazing areas (Tapang 1985:29). The destruction throughout the country played havoc with the national bureaucracy and economy. The destruction in Benguet eliminated official records and offices so that elite families often lost documentation of state title. At the same time, the knowledge and control of elite elders disappeared, as many died under harsh occupation conditions. Post-war political unrest led to new government policies such as the opening of "unimproved public lands" to people for agricultural development (Fry 1983:214). This policy undercut the position of the Ibaloi elite, since much of their land was classified as public.

In Kabayan, post-war developments speeded the elite decline. With the construction of the Ambuklao hydroelectric dam, all land-title processing in the Agno River watershed of the dam was suspended. Nevertheless, improvements to "public" lands continued to be recognized for limited title under the tax-declaration act, which further weakened the control of the cognatic descent group over inherited property by facilitating alienation by individuals. It also allowed the opening of lands along irrigation canals and threatened the social cohesion of irrigation groups. The state did not recognize any property-holding group between the level of the individual and the level of the entire community. Boundary maintenance by property-holding groups such as the bunak or irrigation groups was successfully challenged by other members of the community. Finally, multiple jural levels in Ibaloi society meant that conflict over access to scarce resources was not predictably resolved at the community level. State recognition of communal rights has only exacerbated problems.

A brief example will illustrate what I mean. The mayor, who told us that communal irrigation in Kabayan was supported by the co-operative labour of all community members later admitted to me that there was a lack of "co-operative spirit" when it came to communal self-help projects. He described a situation which developed when a government agency donated eight bags of cement to line a so-called communal irrigation canal:

> At one time I was able to get eight bags of cement which I donated to line that Ensangaey Canal. But the people, when they were assembled to work on that canal, then they asked who would pay for their labour. Can you imagine? To line their own canal? Also, those workers wanted food, cigarettes and even beer! Whenever I try to initiate "self-help" projects here, the people only laugh.

This behaviour is particularly perplexing considering that many people in Kabayan gain access to water based on their interpretation of water as a communal resource. There are several possible explanations for this behaviour.

First and foremost, it must be remembered that irrigation in Kabayan was never a communal project. The mayor did not specify who the people were that were called to work on the proposed canal improvements. They could have been any one of a number of types of participants in irrigated agriculture. Much of the day-to-day maintenance labour and irrigation management along a canal is carried out by the workers on the land, who are often tenants, relatives or people renting land from the actual owners. Improvements over and above regular maintenance work on the system, however, are viewed as the responsibility of the actual landowners. Tenants would view the mayor's proposal as a situation in which their labour was being demanded without normal compensation. In traditional extra-household labour exchanges, it is customary to provide a significant mid-day meal, a few cigarettes and some drinks as the worker's payment. Furthermore, in co-operative irrigation work, when landholders along the canal do not send a representative to join in the group labour, they are sometimes fined the cash or food and drink necessary to provide a meal for the ones who do the work. In the light of such information, the actions of those recruited to work on Ensangaey Canal improvements may be very logical, depending on their status vis-à-vis the land and the irrigation group.

There are many types of appropriators drawing water from irrigation canals today, and ambiguity leads to opportunism, which Ostrom (1990:35) defines as "self-interest with guile." For example, people who opened new paddies along pre-existing irrigation canals often argue that they are not responsible for improvements to an infrastructure in which they have no tenure. Some even refuse to do regular maintenance labour, arguing that their paddies are small and that they only receive water on the suffrage of the own-

ers of the system, which can be revoked at any time. The original paddy owners, of course, argue that those who benefit should make contributions. Each
side views the other as wanting to both ''have their cake and eat it too.''
Finally, even landowners along Ensangaey Canal may have looked askance at
working to install the cement if they calculated that eight bags of cement
were not likely to improve much of one of the longest canals in Kabayan.
Many tail-enders probably doubted that their land would see any benefit.

Kabayan irrigation groups do not represent one of those successful, sustainable cases discussed by Ostrom (1990). There is no local authority solving problems of resource allocation among community members (see also
Grossi 1981). Further, boundary maintenance is impossible, primarily because of problems with defining ''excess water.'' Conklin writes that, among
the Ifugao, if A builds a canal to his plot and B later opens a field between the
source and A's plot, then:

> B may tap into the channel only by making payment (*adang*), usually in
> pigs, to A and by agreeing to share the upkeep of the channel. With time,
> the original ownership may become hard to trace. Even where it is well
> known, old rights of appropriation become weaker than those of validation
> by active repair and contributory labour.

Both the Ifugao and Ibaloi appear to have problems in controlling the number
of beneficiaries along one canal. While the Bontok do not tolerate interference between a source and a long-standing irrigation area (Prill-Brett, pers.
comm.) they have similar problems with excess water flowing away from an
irrigation system (Prill-Brett 1983). I outlined in Chapter Four how conflicts
of this type were resolved in Kabayan through the use of water rotation and
water-distribution practices. But boundary problems remain.

Jural issues remain central to most resource-allocation problems in
Kabayan. Any future attempts by the national government to provide development assistance to these supposedly communal people are going to run into
a veritable rat's nest of tenure and group-membership disputes. Part of the
problem, of course, is that the communal concept has received considerable
reinforcement from government officials and bureaucracy. It also has some
validity from the indigenous point of view, since many resources in the traditional Ibaloi community were shared and controlled by large groups of
people. However, under the indigenous system, the local use group was also
the cultural group—generating norms and rules which prevented opportunism, free riders and misappropriation. While this is still true of some Cordilleran communities, the Kabayan situation is instructive of future problems as
political incorporation and economic integration proceed.

The jural realm of the Ibaloi has been substantially changed by political
incorporation. The competition for control of the gold trade and for the

chiefly positions of the baknang created schisms in Ibaloi society which provided a wedge for the introduction of external jural concepts. In the resulting struggles over resources, some people of Kabayan found advantage in introducing new concepts of rights in resources, while others conserved what local jural autonomy remained and manipulated a simplified discrepancy between local and state jural codes. A more recent concept which has found favour among local strategists is that of communal resources. Here, too, different kinds of actors are involved in the introduction and use of this concept. The landless have used it to win ground against the former elite, but in the larger issue of jurisdiction, which is central to any future local control over property resources, the elite are marketing the idea to the wider Philippine society.

As long as the people of Kabayan must deal with less than full state recognition of local-generated rules of practice (whether traditional or recent inventions with wide local support) at the same time that they are refused the full placement of bureaucratic supports for state tenure regulations, conflict will continue to be a serious impediment to economic development in this region. Under the government of Cory Aquino, conservative forces continued to successfully resist substantive change in the state strategy towards minority groups. Despite the fact that the new state constitution, ratified under Aquino's government, established semi-autonomy for the Cordillera Central, there is no increased security for indigenous land tenure or increased local jural control. In the drafting of the *Organic Act*, which defined the operation of this semi-autonomous region, certain key phrases were introduced before it could be pushed through the national congress (see Wiber and Prill-Brett 1991). These changes made all legislation in certain key areas of property control and resource development in the autonomous zone subject to ''national law.'' How can a group be given ''autonomy'' without the secure control of resources on which to base it? It is no wonder, therefore, that in the 1990 referendum to decide which regions of the Cordillera would participate in the semi-autonomous zone, five of the six political units involved voted against inclusion. It is predictable that under these conditions, local control of resources will remain a problem and that legal pluralism will continue to offer local actors one resource in trying to gain this control.

This chapter began by stressing the importance of investigating the possibility of conflicting jural orders in any analysis of property relations. It then went on to examine the development and operation of multiple sources of jural authority in Kabayan and their role in the competitive economic strategies of individuals. This led to the question of the origin of competing economic interests in Ibaloi society, which was addressed through an historic analysis of the transformation of the Ibaloi economy. The chapter concluded with an investigation of present directions in Kabayan, including a discussion of the rise of ''ethnic communalism'' in the core/periphery power struggles of the Cordillera and the Philippine state. Playing two competing sources of jural authority against one another has had obvious benefits for some Ibaloi, and this is suggestive of the ubiquity of this behaviour in human societies. We need to further explore this idea in future research.

EIGHT

Conclusions

This book documents changes to Ibaloi society, economy and property laws over the past several centuries, and as such, uncovers "the social logic of transformations" (Moore 1986:321). While political incorporation into a nation state (whether independent or colonial) has played a significant part in those transformations, the processes have not been uni-directional. Understanding those processes and their impact on local property control in Kabayan has required an investigation of the heuristic notion that law is pluralistic in many social contexts. Since the concept of pluralistic normative orders has many theoretical implications for the ongoing anthropological concern to understand the relationship between structure and process, the analysis of Kabayan property relations suggests problems with anthropological epistemology which, for the most part, are beyond the scope of this book. None of these epistemological issues are particularly new, but this book provides empirical data which supports recent challenges to anthropological methodology and suggests directions for fruitful future research.

This book does address methodological problems. For example, what is meant by terms such as communal, corporate or co-operative? and, an equally important question, are they applicable to property relations in non-Western societies? Despite detailed and careful ethnographies to the contrary, cultures of the Philippine Cordillera are categorized as practising bilateral descent and are also widely characterized as being communal in their property relations, especially in regards to irrigation. But the irrigation systems in Kabayan are not communal at all, neither in the general sense that most members of the community have rights in them, nor in any more specific sense such that community authorities manage resource use. In fact, kinship has played a more important role in the property system, in recruitment to property-based groups, in the organization of those groups, and in the assignment of status within them. Principles of group organization must be a matter of more careful empirical investigation, particularly in relation to membership recruitment, boundary maintenance, the allocation of rights and the generation of rules. Common interest, social rank and relative rates of investment have all played a role in forming productive groups among the Ibaloi. Among the kadangyan in Ibaloi society, alliance networks and co-operative joint-venture organizations were often couched in kinship terms, but common interest and social background were actually more important than descent or affinity. In the irrigation systems of Kabayan, leadership relies on multi-strand relationships to other members of the group, including kin, landlord, respected elder and municipal official. The indiscriminate application of the communal concept in upland communities of the Cordillera Central has increased boundary-maintenance problems, in that the actions of individuals formerly designated as non-members have been allowed to undercut the rights of those within property-holding groups.

George Appell (1974, 1976) has attempted to address the inadequate nomenclature employed in the comparative study of property systems. While his work is important, it requires elaboration. The problem is tied to questions of scientific method in general. As van Benthem van den Bergh (1986) has recently reiterated, a focus on cause and a tendency to test for causation by holding constant a large number of variables leads to simplism. In the sciences, where good results were originally obtained using this approach, the inadequacies of the method become apparent as more complex phenomenon are addressed. In the social sciences, results have always been unsatisfactory, with unfortunate results for our credibility.

Misnomers applied to Cordilleran cultures find a source not only in our kinship theory, with the simplistic contrast of bilateral versus unilineal, but also in a generalized West versus the Rest approach (*cf.* Goody 1990). We see this problem not only in the terms we apply to others but also in the way we characterize ourselves through contrast with them. The property-holding patterns labelled corporate and communal, correlates of unilineal versus bilateral, allow us to contrast non-Western societies with the supposedly individualistic Western world (see Grossi 1981). Settling on definitions in the field of law entails similar processes. When our nomenclature is inadequate to the cross-cultural complexity of empirical observations, those observations can only be discussed by cramming them into concepts that don't quite fit. An example is the loose way in which property-use rights are discussed using terms such as owner, usufruct, fee simple and others, without empirical justification. In comparative cross-cultural studies, the resulting misrepresentation has affected our understanding of all parties concerned, ourselves as well as the "significant other" with whom we intrinsically contrast ourselves. In defining ourselves through opposition to some other, whether favourably or unfavourably, the errors have been compounded, so that I suspect the adequacy of such terms to encompass what we experience in our own culture. And since ideas have an impact on behaviour, oversimplified concepts inevitably find their expression in the realm of practice, which in time, has its own behavioural and theoretical ramifications.

While the tendency to simplism in describing property relations has been a serious handicap to comparative studies, a proliferation of such concepts does not solve the problem. While I found George Appell's methodology for the identification of property-owning social entities very useful for discerning how property-holding groups are organized, how the rights in property are distributed among the membership and where conflicts may arise, I also found that it relies on assumptions about legal institutions which may not be warranted. In neglecting and misunderstanding the role of law, we have misunderstood diachronic processes in property systems. Thus our end goal of understanding emergent structure is imperilled. How and why property systems change over time is tied up with legal strategies. From this perspective, Appell's approach does not go far enough in focussing on a few key variables.

We must place more emphasis on the questions raised by the existence of pluralism in most human societies. These two issues, the diachronic perspective and pluralism, are related. For example, it is obvious from a diachronic analysis of Ibaloi property systems that external agencies, such as the Spanish or the American colonial bureaucracies, were not in the position to have controlled the outcome of changes to indigenous Philippine upland cultures and their property systems. The role of individual actors and interest groups within Ibaloi society was at least as important as colonial governmental policy and economic initiatives. In order to better understand the forces which influenced the behaviour of these individuals and groups in relation to productive resources, it is useful to turn to the potential for building discrepancy in the contrast between jural concepts. The material from this analysis suggests that in any situation where such a discrepancy exists, it will play a central role in human purposive strategy. In most societies, there are conflicting interests which benefit from and therefore promote (and even invent) the flexibility inherent in a situation of legal pluralism. Such interests must be the focus of more research which does not prejudge the nature and outcome of the economic strategies of individuals. Among the Ibaloi, gold miners and traders created a normative order which their descendants subverted through the introduction of external property concepts. These people, in turn, had their economic advantages undercut when external conceptualizations of indigenous practice were used by other local people to further their goals. As van Benthem van den Bergh suggests, in abandoning a "blame orientation"

in social science, we will often find ourselves tracing the unintended consequences of individual behaviour patterns.

This leads us full circle to the question of multiple normative orders and
their correlation with social stratification and political interests. Merry (1988)
identifies two strains of research in legal pluralism, the "classical," which
focusses on situations of "imposed law," and the "new," which looks at the
pluralism inherent in all complex societies. I agree with Benda-Beckmann
(1988), who rejects this as misleading. In reference to the ground-breaking
work of Moore with her "semi-autonomous fields," he (ibid.:899) writes:

> The strength of Moore's article also did not lie in the fact that she proved
> legal pluralism, but in that she showed how in everyday relation and inter-
> action networks people generate their own rule system, and in doing so are
> influenced by (a plurality of) rules and institutional elements that have
> been, and continue to be, generated and maintained in other interaction set-
> tings such as law schools, bureaucracies, and courts. Its limitation is not
> that she refused to call the rules of the semiautonomous field legal, but that
> she left open how semiautonomy is established. Is it by normatively
> defined constraints or by interactive constraints (in the name of law) from
> persons inside or outside the interaction network?

The difference between what Merry calls the new and the old legal pluralism
studies is simply that in the colonial setting, the sources of legal pluralism
were assumed to be the imposition of external codes on a formerly independent people. This assumption may be erroneous and overly simplistic. We now
know that the "classical" and the "new" legal pluralism research examines
the same phenomenon. I think it is important to keep in mind that so-called
"customary law" is a growing and changing normative and ideological
order, just as state law must be, with no less a tendency towards the "totalitarian ideal" identified by Vanderlinden (1989:153). And if customary law is
of the same phenomena as state law, then processes affecting the one cannot
fail to exist relative to the other.

Investigating pluralism is building on Appell's attempt to understand
"emergent" structures in society. The role of the decisions and actions of
individual actors can be seen to be central to the purposive seeking out of
alternatives in the "opportunity structure." As F. von Benda-Beckmann
(1983) suggests, plurality provides the necessary leeway for individual actors
or interest groups to lift behaviour out of the opportunity structure and reify it
in the social structure. If state law had not come along in Ibaloi history,
people may have had to invent some other contrasting normative order to
serve their changing purposes. Indeed, they did so anyway, in that they
created a totalitarian normative order involving ritual imperatives (see Wiber
1989) of a degree and kind not seen elsewhere in the Cordillera. The uses to
which the Ibaloi poor have subsequently put academic and bureaucratic mis-

conceptions of Ibaloi custom points to the utility of alternative normative orders for all strata of society, whatever their source. The question of emergent structure hinges on purposive political and economic actions. Because of this, we must be very aware of the specific opportunities, interest groups, goals and strategies of the various political actors within the social structure and within the opportunity structure—at the present time, and in the past.

This point leads to practical considerations for research in the development context. Today, any individual working on issues with any connection to property issues (and what has not?) will sooner or later have to cope with the existence of some level of plural jural operations. Multiple normative levels exist in former colonies, in peasant societies, and in tribal or minority areas of all nation states. Merely acknowledging these levels and trying to decide which of them has some sort of moral superiority will not solve the problem. The effect of the purposive action of individuals in the creation, exploitation and reinforcement of the plural jural situation requires more research. Vanderlinden (1989) suggests that the place to look for answers is in the networks which generate normative orders. One caution is that we cannot assume these networks persist as cohesive groups or consciously operate using law as an instrument in their repertoire. Events in Kabayan suggest the importance of individual innovation and the tendency of some to mimic what has been successful for others, without realizing the wider consequences of their actions. In the context of economic development, the need to keep this in mind is as important for formal social engineering planned and implemented by bureaucratic agencies as it is for the analysis of local behaviour. Each will have their unintended consequences in the social sphere (see Wiber 1988).

Finally, there are implications in all of this for our continuing attempts to understand the relationship between structure and process. I am not suggesting that society is formless, and is continually being reconstructed as a consequence of the opportunistic behaviour of atomistic individuals. There is obviously a pattern of reacting against patterns more than there is a continual invention of new. In the reaction against structure, there is the implicit leaning on structure which has long been recognized as the strategy of intermediaries. Nor do I intend that we should ignore the relevant issues of external influences. I agree that this tends to make the actor look like the victim of his/her self-made fate (Moore 1986:322). But empirical investigations must begin somewhere, and the methodological and flawed-assumption problems are more comprehensible at the motivated-actor end of the continuum. What is needed now, in addition to methodological rigour, is more empirical investigation into specific contexts of manipulation of societal normative orders and the subsequent change or generation of new forms at what Moore (ibid.:329) has called the ''intermediate level'' of organization and of analysis. The source of alternative ideas and the impact of external influences can be factored in as they are encountered. Only then can we begin to understand the social world as it is experienced and transformed by individual actors. And isn't this the perspective that really counts?

Glossary

aba	also called gabi, a plant with edible root and leaves.
abiteg	the poorer strata in Ibaloi society as opposed to the wealthier landowning strata.
aeshe	fieldhand client in a *kadangyan* household.
ani	harvest.
agi	kin or close relatives
amdag	curative ritual for a minor illness.
angja	sorcerer and recipient of inherited power.
aramag	a long, complex funerary ritual surrounding the death of a person with wealth and prestige.
a'tang	a traditional labour arrangement used specifically in rice production where labour was exchanged for a share in the crop.
ator	Bontok for neighbourhood group cross-cut by patrilineal ties
badiw	traditional chants performed on specific ritual occasions.
baga'en	a slave.
bagodong	to allow something to rot, as with rice stalks pounded into the paddy muds after harvest.
ba'jug	sorcery power which is inherited.
baknang	a position of leadership in an Ibaloi community; achieved only after completing the *peshit* prestige cycle, which is an inherited prerogative of the offspring of kadangyan.
baley'tok	gold deposits or mines.
bingay	the traditional share in the natural increase of animals; given as payment to the caretaker by the owner.
bodusan	property "free for use by everyone."
bu'nung	traditional prayers to the ancestors.
butek	a uniform-sized, harvested bundle of rice panicles; a measurement of payment and a storage unit for rice; it contains approximately five kilos of rice grain.
bwatbwat	the meat portion given to each individual taking part in a *cañao*; at the end of the festivities it is taken home and consumed individually.
camote	a variety of sweet potato (*Ipomoea batatas*) grown as a staple.

143

cañao	the general term for ritualized feasts.
che'ko	a term indicating a certain size of rice field; refers to the fact that there is only "one wall," as in a very small field.
din'teg	Ibaloi term for law, literally "to make straight."
e'so	the traditional relationship between landowner and tenant and specific to rice production where the tenant takes responsibility for production and shares the yield with the landowner.
intugtukan	supreme judicial and political authority for the community (Bontok).
kadangyan	the upper strata in Ibaloi society; people who have the inherited right to perform the *peshit*, or prestige cycle.
kah'dot	the Ibaloi term for a variety of cañao-type rituals.
kait	distant relative.
kalañguyan	a distinct group which occupies the heights above Kabayan Central; has the connotation of "hillbilly" in the community.
ka'pe	a *cañao* instigated by a message from the ancestors; to bring wealth, good luck, or to avoid disaster.
keh'daring	the ancestral spirits.
kaingin	an introduced term frequently used to refer to dry fields in which slash and burn and long fallow is practised. *See also* swidden.
kintoman	traditional varieties of rice; usually with a red or brown appearance to the grain; these varieties are tall, photoperiodic and take approximately seven to eight months to mature.
kiyad	a curative ceremony performed to placate angry ancestors.
kod'dey	a harvest feast which required the ritual closing of the community and the co-operation of all households.
kola'kol	an irrigation canal; to dig or scratch; an awl; the hole made by an auger or drill.
kom'boy	backpacking goods or materials over foot trails in the mountains.
lupon	the short form for *lupong tagapayapa*, or barangay court.
mambunong	the one who will be performing the prayers, or the native priest.
man'dapis	the one who will be distributing the water.
ma'ngi'din'teg	Community elders, "the ones who will make things straight."
na'ama	the respected elders of the community.
namshit	those individuals who formed the elite in Ibaloi society through the successful completion of the peshit, or prestige cycle.
nava	the gold-bearing ore extracted from mines.
o'boan	a traditional form of labour exchange where equal amounts of the same type of labour are exchanged by two or more households.
olnong	meetings to decide on changes to the law.
opo	grave goods; each rank in Ibaloi society has distinctive grave-good requirements.
osaway	"came but went away again."
pagey	rice.
pan'se'jew	gold panning in streams.

pastol	the "cowboy" who looked after the cattle herd of a wealthy family; a "one leg plus" share was received for each animal born to the herd.
payew	irrigated rice land.
peshit	the prestige ritual cycle which required wealth to perform. It involved successive ceremonies of the butchering and distribution of increasing numbers of animals; known as the "rich man's cañao," it was the only legitimate route to the baknang position.
pinat'djan	the funeral cañao (also called ara'mag).
poldeya	cash labour; a practice probably introduced into the mountains by the Spanish; the term is possibly derived from "per dia."
poesto	market stall owner.
sa'je'wan	rectangular sluice box for gold washing.
sari sari	store, a small-scale general store.
sayo	gold mining or panning.
shilos	rituals of the customary religion.
silbi	debt slave.
sinampulo	a curative ceremony where the needs of the ancestors are interpreted and satisfied by the sacrifice of animals.
sitio	a neighbourhood or small settlement within a larger community.
somjang	counter-sorcery curative ceremony.
swidden	dry gardens planted on the hillsides after burning off the natural vegetation. *See also* kaingin.
talek'bed	a place where water wells up with sufficient force that it can be tapped for an irrigation canal headwater.
talon	varieties of rice which are grown in the wet season; they generally are non-photoperiodic, dwarf, white-rice varieties.
tapey	rice wine; the sacred drink of ceremonies.
tar'oy	a hollow bamboo or pine log which is used to transfer irrigation water over obstacles or ravines.
ta'yaw	traditional dancing performed only at cañao.
temo	a curative ritual required to appease the ancestors and cure a form of violent derangement.
ten'neng	a term indicating a size of rice paddy; denotes a larger size since it refers to "three walls."
tong tong	dispute-resolution hearings moderated by respected elders.
uma	the non-irrigated gardens planted on steep slopes surrounding the community during the rainy season. *See also* swidden and kaingin.

References

Afrika Instituut Leiden. 1951. *Land Tenure Symposium, Amsterdam 1950.* Leiden: Universitaire Pers Leiden.

Anderson, James N. 1987. "Lands at Risk, People at Risk: Perspectives on Tropical Forest Transformations in the Philippines." In *Lands at Risk in the Third World: Local Level Perspectives*, edited by Peter D. Little and Michael Horowitz, 249-68. Boulder: Westview Press.

Appell, George. 1974. The Analysis of Property Systems: The Creation and Devolution of Property Interests Among the Rungus of Borneo. Prepared for the 1974 Conference of the Association of Social Anthropologists on Social Anthropology and Law, University of Keele, 27-30 March, 1974.

————. 1976. "The Rungus: Social Structure in a Cognatic Society and Its Ritual Symbolization." In *The Societies of Borneo: Explanations in the Theory of Cognatic Social Structure*, edited by George Appell, 66-86. Special Publication of the American Anthropological Association No. 6. Washington.

————. 1980. Epistemological Issues in Anthropological Inquiry: Social Structuralism, Cognitive Structuralism, Synthetic Structuralism and Opportunism. Parts I and II. *Canberra Anthropology* 3:1-27 and 4:1-22.

————. 1984. Methodological Issues in the Corporation Redux. *American Ethnologist* 11:815-17.

Aranal-Sereno, Ma. Lourdes, and Roan Libarios. 1983. The Interface Between National Land Law and Kalinga Land Law. *Philippine Law Journal* 58:420-56.

Arno, Andrew. 1985. Structural Communication and Control Communication: An Interactionist Perspective on Legal and Customary Procedures for Conflict Management. *American Anthropologist* 87:40-55.

Bacdayan, Albert. 1976. "From Isolation to Articulation: The Barrio Charter and Social Change in Northern Philippines." In *Culture Change in the Philippines*, 1-17. Williamsburg: College of William and Mary, Studies in Third World Societies, Publication No. 1.

_____. 1980. "Mountain Irrigators in the Philippines." In *Irrigation and Agricultural Development in Asia*, edited by E. Walter Coward, Jr., 172-85. Ithaca: Cornell University Press.

Bacoling, William T. 1984. Legally Yours: Sadiay E Dinteg Ja Kuansia. *A Periodic Report from the Office of the Provincial Attorney, Benguet Province* 1(4):9-10.

Bagadion, Benjamin. 1988. "The Evolution of the Policy Context: An Historical Overview." In *Transforming A Bureaucracy,* edited by F. Korten and R. Siy, 1-19. Manila: Ateneo de Manila Press.

_____, and Frances Korten. 1980. Developing Viable Irrigators' Associations: Lessons from Small Scale Irrigation Development for the Philippines. *Agricultural Administration* 7:273-87.

Bagamaspad, Anavic, and Z. Hamada-Pawid. 1985. *A People's History of Benguet.* Baguio City: Baguio Printing and Publishing.

Barnes, J.A. 1969. "The Politics of Law." In *Man in Africa,* edited by Mary Douglas and P. Kaberry, 99-118. London: Tavistock Publishers.

Barnett, Milton. 1967. "Subsistence and Transition of Agricultural Development among the Ibaloi." In *Studies in Philippine Anthropology,* edited by Mario D. Zamora, 299-323. Quezon City: Alemar Pheonix.

Barton, R.F. 1949. *The Kalingas. Their Institutions and Custom Law.* Chicago: University of Chicago Press.

_____. 1969. [1919]. *Ifugao Law.* Berkeley: University of California Press.

Bastin, John. 1954. *The Development of Raffles' Ideas on the Land Rent System in Java and the Work of the Mackenzie Land Tenure Commission.* s'-Gravenhage: N.V. De Nederlandse Bock-En Steendrukbery v.h. H.L. Smits.

Befu, H., and L. Plotnicov. 1962. Types of Corporate Unilineal Descent Groups. *American Anthropologist* 64:313-27.

Behar, Ruth. 1984. The Web of Use-Rights: Forms and Conceptions of Communal Property among Leonese Labradores. *Anthropological Quarterly* 57:71-82.

Bell, Diane. 1983. Going It Alone: Practising Applied Anthropology. *Anthropological Forum* 5:176-81.

Bello, Moises. 1972. *Kankanay Social Organization and Culture Change.* Community Development Research Council, University of the Philippines PACD-UP Project.

Benda-Beckmann, Franz von. 1979. *Property in Social Continuity.* The Hague: Martinus Nijhoff.

_____. 1983. Why Law Does Not Behave: Critical and Constructive Reflections on the Social Scientific Perception of the Social Significance of Law. Vol. 1. Compiled by Harald W. Finkler, 233-62. *Proceedings of the Folk Law and Legal Pluralism Commission Symposia, XIth International Conference of Anthropological and Ethnological Sciences, Vancouver, Canada, August 19-23.*

_____. 1986. "Anthropology and Comparative Law." In *Anthropology of Law in the Netherlands*, edited by K. von Benda-Beckmann and Fons Strijbosch. Dordrecht: Foris Publications.

_____. 1988. Comment on Merry. *Law and Society Review* 22 (5):897-901.

_____. 1989. Scapegoat and Magic Charm: Law in Development Theory and Practise. *Journal of Legal Pluralism* 28:129-48.

Benda-Beckmann, Keebet von. 1983. The Implementation of State Court Decisions in West-Sumatra, Indonesia Minangkabau Land Disputes. Vol. 1. Compiled by Harald W. Finkler, 14-59. *Proceedings of the Folk Law and Legal Pluralism Commission Symposia, XIth International Congress of Anthropological and Ethnological Sciences, Vancouver, Canada, August 19-23.*

_____. 1984. *The Broken Stairways to Consensus: Village Courts and State Justice in Minangkabau.* Dordrecht: Foris Publications.

_____, and Fons Strijbosch, eds. 1986. *Anthropology of Law in the Netherlands.* Dordrecht: Foris Publications.

Benguet Socio-Economic Profile. 1981. Baguio: Baguio Printing and Publishing.

Benthem van den Bergh, Godfried van. 1986. "The Improvement of Human Means of Orientation: Towards Synthesis in the Social Sciences." In *Development Studies: Critique and Renewal*, edited by R. Apthorpe and A. Krahl, 109-35. Leiden: E. J. Brill.

Berkes, Fikret, ed. 1989. *Common Property Resources: Ecology and Community-based Sustainable Development.* London: Belhaven Press.

_____, and M. Farvar. 1989. "Introduction and Overview." In *Common Property Resources*, edited by F. Berkes, 1-17. London: Bellhaven Press.

Blair, Emma H., and James Robertson. 1973. *The Philippine Islands 1493-1848*, 55 vol. Mandaluyon, Rizal: Cachos Hermandos.

Botengan, Kate. 1976. *Bontoc Lifeways: A Study in Education and Culture.* Manila: Capital Publishing House, Centro Escolar University.

Bowen, John R. 1986. On the Political Construction of Tradition: *Gotong Royong* in Indonesia. *Journal of Asian Studies* 45(3):545-61.

_____. 1988. The Transformation of an Indonesian Property System: Adat, Islam and Social Change in the Gayo Highlands. *American Ethnologist* 15:274.

Bromley, Daniel W. 1989. *Economic Interests and Institutions: The Conceptual Foundations of Public Policy.* New York: Basil Blackwell.

Brown, D.E. 1974. Corporations and Social Classification. *Current Anthropology* 15:29-52.

_____. 1976. *Principles of Social Structure: Southeast Asia.* London: Westview Press.

_____. 1984. More on Corporations. *American Ethnologist* 11:813-15.

Brush, Stephen B. 1977. *Mountain, Field and Family: The Economy and Human Ecology of an Andean Valley.* Philadelphia: University of Pennsylvania Press.

Burman, Sandra, and B. Harrell-Bond. 1979. *The Imposition of Law*. New York: Academic Press.

Burns, Peter. 1989. The Myth of Adat. *Journal of Legal Pluralism* 28:1-127.

Chanok, Martin. 1985. *Law, Custom and Social Order: The Colonial Experience in Malawi and Zambia*. Cambridge: Cambridge University Press.

Cochraine, Glynn. 1971. The Use of the Concept of ''Corporation.'' *American Anthropologist* 73:1144-55.

Collins, Hugh. 1982. *Marxism and Law*. Oxford: Clarendon Press.

Comaroff, John L., and Simon Roberts. 1981. *Rules and Processes*. Chicago: University of Chicago Press.

Commission on Folk Law and Legal Pluralism. 1983. *Proceedings of the Symposia on Folk Law and Legal Pluralism, XIth International Conference of Anthropological and Ethnological Sciences, Vancouver, Canada, August 19-23, 1983*. Harald W. Finkler, compiler. Department of Indian Affairs and Northern Development Publication.

Commission on Folk Law and Legal Pluralism. 1991. *Proceedings of the VIth International Symposium, Commission on Folk Law and Legal Pluralism, Ottawa, Canada, August 14-18, 1990*. Harald W. Finkler, compiler. Department of Indian Affairs and Northern Development Publication.

Conklin, Harold. 1980. *Ethnographic Atlas of the Ifugao*. New Haven: Yale University Press.

Cruz, Ma. Conception, L.B. Cornista and D.C. Dayan. 1987. *Legal and Institutional Issues of Irrigation Water Rights in the Philippines*. Laguna, Philippines: Agrarian Reform Institute, University of the Philippines at Los Baños.

Dagmar, Hans. 1983. Planning for Aboriginal Social Change: The Role of Cultural Identity. *Anthropological Forum* 5:208-20.

Dahlberg, Kenneth. 1979. *Beyond the Green Revolution*. New York: Plenum Press.

Dart, Donn V. 1977. *Compadrinazgo: Ritual Kinship in the Philippines*. DeKalb: Northern Illinois University Press.

Davenport, William H. 1959. Nonunilineal Descent and Descent Groups. *American Anthropologist* 61:557-72.

Davis, William G. 1973. *Social Relations in a Philippine Market*. Berkeley: University of California Press.

————. 1978. Anthropology and Theories of Modernization: Some Perspectives from Benguet. *Papers in Anthropology* 19:59-72.

Dove, Michael. 1982. ''The Myth of the Communal Longhouse in Rural Development.'' In *Too Rapid Rural Development*, edited by Colin MacAndrews and L.S. Chin, 14-78. Athens: Ohio University Press.

————. 1986. Peasant Versus Government Perception and Use of the Environment: A Case-study of Banjarese Ecology and River Basin Development in South Kalimantan. *Journal of Southeast Asian Studies* 17(1):113-36.

Dow, James. 1973. On the Muddled Concept of Corporation in Anthropology. *American Anthropologist* 75:904-908.

Dozier, Edward. 1967. *The Kalinga of Northern Luzon, Philippines*. New York: Holt, Rinehart and Winston.

Durrenberger, E. Paul. 1984. *Chayanov, Peasants, and Economic Anthropology*. New York: Academic Press.

Drucker, Charles B. 1977. To Inherit the Land: Descent and Decision in Northern Luzon. *Ethnology* 16:1-20.

Eggan, Fred. 1963. Cultural Drift and Social Change. *Current Anthropologist* 4:347-53.

————. 1967. "Some Aspects of Bilateral Social Systems in the Northern Philippines." In *Studies in Philippine Anthropology*, edited by Mario D. Zamora, 186-201. Quezon City: Alemar Phoenix.

Ember, Melvin. 1959. The Nonunilineal Descent Groups of Samoa. *American Anthropologist* 61:573-77.

Feder, Gershon, and Tongroj Onchan. 1987. Land Ownership Security and Farm Investment in Thailand. *American Journal of Agricultural Economics* 69(2):311-20.

Feeny, David. 1977. *From Property Rights in Man to Property Rights in Land: Institutional Change in Thai Agriculture, 1850 to 1949*. Department of Economics Working Paper No. 11-12. Hamilton, Ontario: McMaster University.

Fiagoy, Geraldine. 1985. *Resource Use in Loo Valley*. Gran Cordillera Institutional Publication of the Cordillera Studies Center No. 1. Baguio City: University of the Philippines, pp. 16-19.

Firth, Raymond. 1957. A Note on Descent Groups in Polynesia. *Man* 57:4-8.

Frank, Andre G. 1969. *Capitalism and Underdevelopment in Latin America*. New York and London: Monthly Review Press.

Fry, Howard. 1983. *A History of the Mountain Province*. Quezon City: New Day Publishers.

Gailey, Christine Ward. 1985. The Kindness of Strangers: Transformations of Kinship in Precapitalist Class and State Formation. *Culture* 5:3-16.

Galanter, Marc. 1981. Justice in Many Rooms. *Journal of Legal Pluralism* 19:1-47.

Giddons, Anthony. 1984. *The Constitution of Society: Outline of a Theory of Structuration*. Cambridge: University of Cambridge Press.

Gilbert, Dennis. 1981. Cognatic Descent Groups in Upper-class Lima (Peru). *American Ethnologist* 8:739-57.

Glick, Thomas. 1970. *Irrigation and Society in Medieval Valencia*. Cambridge: Belknap Press of Harvard.

Goodell, Grace E. 1984. Bugs, Bunds, Banks and Bottlenecks: Organizational Contradictions in the New Rice Technology. *Economic Development and Cultural Change* 33:23-41.

————. 1985. Paternalism, Patronage and Potlatch: The Dynamics of Giving and Being Given To. *Current Anthropology* 26:247-66.

Goodenough, Ward H. 1955. A Problem in Malayo-Polynesian Social Organization. *Current Anthropology* 57:71-83.

————. 1961. Review of *Social Structure in Southeast Asia* edited by George Peter Murdock. *American Anthropologist* 63:1341-47.

————. 1971. "Corporations": Reply to Cochrane. *American Anthropologist* 73:1150-52.

Goody, Jack. 1983. *The Development of Family and Marriage in Europe*. Cambridge: Cambridge University Press.

————. 1990. *The Oriental, the Ancient and the Primitive*. Cambridge: Cambridge University Press.

Greenwood, Davydd J. 1976. *Unrewarding Wealth. The Commercialization and Collapse of Agriculture in a Spanish Basque Town*. Cambridge: Cambridge University Press.

Gregory, C.A. 1982. *Gifts and Commodities*. London: Academic Press.

Griffiths, John. 1986. What is Legal Pluralism? *Journal of Legal Pluralism* 24:1-55.

Grossi, Paolo. 1981. *An Alternative to Private Property. Collective Property in the Juridical Consciousness of the Nineteenth Century*, translated by Lydia G. Cochrane. Chicago: University of Chicago Press.

Guy, George. 1958. The Economic Life of the Mountain Tribes of Northern Luzon, Philippines. *Journal of East Asiatic Studies* 7:1-38.

Halperin, Rhoda H. 1988. *Economies Across Cultures. Towards a Comparative Science of the Economy*. New York: St. Martin's Press.

Hayden, Robert M. 1987. Turn-taking, Overlap, and the Task at Hand: Ordering Speaking Turns in Legal Settings. *American Ethnologist* 14(2):251-70.

Holleman, J.F. 1986. "Trouble-cases and Trouble-less Cases in the Study of Customary Law and Legal Reform." In *Anthropology of Law in the Netherlands*, edited by K. von Benda-Beckmann and Fons Strijbosch, 110-31. Dordrecht: Foris Publications.

Hollnsteiner, Mary. 1963. *The Dynamics of Power in a Philippine Municipality*. Quezon City: University of the Philippines, Diliman.

————, ed. 1979. "Reciprocity as a Filipino Value." In *Society, Culture and the Filipino*, 38-43. Quezon City: The Institute of Philippine Culture, Ateneo de Manila.

Hunt, Alan. 1985. The Ideology of Law: Advances and Problems in Recent Applications of the Concept of Ideology to the Analysis of Law. *Law and Society Review* 19:11-37.

Jenks, Albert. 1905. *The Bontok Igorot*. Department of the Interior, Ethnological Survey Publications Vol. 7. Manila: Bureau of Public Printing.

Jensen, Irene. 1975. *The Chinese in the Philippines during the American Regime: 1898-1946.* Saratoga, California: R. and E. Research Association Publishers.

Keesing, Felix. 1949. Notes on Bontoc Social Organization, Northern Philippines. *American Anthopologist* 51:578-601.

_____. 1962. *The Ethnohistory of Northern Luzon.* Stanford: Stanford University Press.

_____, and Marie Keesing. 1934. *Taming Philippine Headhunters.* London: George Allen and Unwin.

Keith, Emma. 1963. Some Aspects of the Daily Life of the Caponga Ibaloys as Reflected in their Folklore. Master's thesis. Philippine Women's University.

Kidder, R. 1979. "Toward an Integrated Theory of Imposed Law." In *The Imposition of Law*, edited by S. Burman and B. Harrell-Bond. New York: Academic Press.

Kladze, A.K.P. 1983. "The Effect of the Interaction Between State Law and Customary Law in Ghana." Vol. 1. Compiled by Harald W. Finkler. *Proceedings of the Folk Law and Legal Pluralism Commission Symposia, XIth International Congress of Anthropological and Ethnological Sciences, Vancouver, Canada, August 19-23.*

Korten, Frances F., and Robert Y. Siy, Jr. 1988. *Transforming a Bureaucracy. The Experience of the Philippine National Irrigation Administration.* Manila: Ateneo de Manila Press.

Lam, Marion. 1983. The Imposition of Anglo-American Laws of Land Tenure on Hawaiians. Vol. 1. Compiled by Harald W. Finkler, 233-62. *Proceedings of the Folk Law and Legal Pluralism Commission Symposia, XIth International Conference of Anthropological and Ethnological Sciences, Vancouver, Canada, August 19-23.*

Lawless, Robert. 1978. Impinging Extra-Kalinga Forces and Change in Pasil Municipality. *Papers in Anthropology* 19:145-59.

Leach, E.R. 1961. *Rethinking Anthropology.* London: The Athlone Press.

Leano, Isabel W. 1958. The Ibalois of Takdian. Their Social, Economic and Religious Life. Master's thesis. Philippine Women's University.

Ledec, George. 1985. "The Political Economy of Tropical Deforestation." In *Divesting Nature's Capital*, edited by Leonard H. Jeffry, 179-226. New York: Holmes and Meier.

Lewis, Henry T. 1971. *Ilocano Rice Farmers.* Honolulu: University of Hawaii Press.

_____. 1978. Ilocano Behavior, Social Organization, and Change. *Papers in Anthropology* 19(1):133-44.

_____. 1991. *Ilocano Irrigation. The Corporate Resolution.* Asian Studies at Hawaii, No. 37. University of Hawaii Press.

Lewis, Martin W. 1992. *Wagering the Land. Ritual, Capital, and Environmental Degradation in the Cordillera of Northern Luzon, 1900-1986.* Berkeley: University of California Press.

Lizarondo, Mario, Zenaida de la Cruz, and Taciana Valdellon. 1979. *A Socio-Economic Study of Vegetable Farmers in Benguet.* Agricultural Marketing Report Series, Vol. 1, No. 4. Quezon City: Bureau of Agricultural Economics.

Long, Norman. 1986. "Introduction." In *The Commoditization Debate: Labour Process, Strategy and Social Network*, edited by Norman Long, Jan Douwe van der Ploeg, Chris Curtin and Louk Box, 1-123. Agricultural University Wageningen.

Lopez, Maria Elena. 1987. "The Politics of Land at Risk in the Philippine Frontier." In *Lands at Risk in the Third World: Local Level Perspectives*, edited by Peter D. Little and Michael Horowitz, 230-48. Boulder: Westview Press.

Lopez-Gonzaga, Violeta. 1983. *Peasants in the Hills: A Study of the Dynamics of Social Change among the Buhid Swidden Cultivators in the Philippines.* Quezon City: University of the Philippines Press, Diliman.

Lynch, Frank. 1979. "Big and Little People: Social Class in the Rural Philippines." In *Society, Culture and the Filipino*, edited by Mary R. Hollnsteiner, 44-48. Quezon City: The Institute of Philippine Culture. Ateneo de Manila University.

Lynch, Owen, Jr. 1983. A Survey of Research on Upland Tenure and Displacement. Presented to the National Conference on Research in the Uplands, Diliman University, Quezon City, April 11.

Lyon, Margo L. 1970. *Bases of Conflict in Rural Java.* Berkeley: University of California Press.

Maine, Sir Henry S. 1890. *Village-Communities in the East and West.* London: John Murray.

————. 1901 [1881]. *Ancient Law.* London: John Murray.

Merry, Sally. 1988. Legal Pluralism. *Law and Society Review* 22(5):869-96.

Money, J.W.B. 1861. *Java. Or How to Manage a Colony*, vol. 1. London: Hurst and Blackett Publishing.

Moore, Sally Falk. 1978. *Law as Process.* London: Routledge and Kegan Paul.

————. 1986. *Social Facts and Fabrications. "Customary" Law on Kilimanjaro 1880-1980.* Cambridge: Cambridge University Press.

Morse, Bradford W. 1984. *Aboriginal Peoples and the Law.* Carleton: Carleton University Press.

Moss, C.R. 1919. *Nabaloi Law and Ritual.* Publications in American Archaeology and Ethnology, edited by A.L. Kroeber, vol. 15:208-35. Berkeley: University of California Press.

————, and A.L. Kroeber. 1919. *Nabaloi Songs.* Publications in American Archaeology and Ethnology, edited by A.L. Kroeber, vol 15:187-206. Berkeley: University of California Press.

Murdock, G.P. 1960. "Cognatic Forms of Social Organization." In *Social Structure in Southeast Asia*, edited by G.P. Murdock, 1-14. Chicago: Quadrangle Books.

————. 1964. The Kindred. *American Anthropologist* 66:129-31.

Nader, Laura, and Duane Metzger. 1963. Conflict Resolution in Two Mexican Communities. *American Anthropologist* 65:584-92.

Newman, Kathrine S. 1983. *Law and Economic Organization. A Comparative Study of Preindustrial Societies.* Cambridge: Cambridge University Press.

Noricks, Jay Smith. 1983. Unrestricted Cognatic Descent and Corporateness on Niutao, a Polynesian Island of Tuvala. *American Ethnological Society* 3: 571-84.

Ostrom, Elinor. 1990. *Governing the Commons. The Evolution of Institutions for Collective Action.* Cambridge: Cambridge University Press.

Philippines Today. n.d. *National Issue on the National Economic and Development Authority (NEDA) Development Strategy.* Baguio: Baguio Printing.

Pospisil, Leopold. 1958. *Kapauku Papuans and Their Law.* New Haven: Yale University Press.

————. 1967. Legal Levels and Multiplicity of Legal Systems in Human Societies. *Journal of Conflict Resolution* 11:2-26.

————. 1971. *Anthropology of Law: A Comparative Theory.* New York: Harper & Row.

Prill-Brett, June. 1975. Bontok Warfare. Master's thesis. University of the Philippines.

————. 1983. The Social Dynamics of Irrigation in Tukukan Society. *The Cordillera Social Science Monograph Series* 2:1-47.

————. 1985. Bontok Land Resource and Management. Presented to the Second SUAN-EAPI Regional Research Symposium, Baguio City, Philippines. 18-22 March 1985. Sponsored by the Southeast Asian Universities Agroecosystem Network and the East-West Center Environment and Policy Institute.

————. 1986. "The Bontok: Traditional Wet-Rice and Swidden Cultivators of the Philippines." In *Traditional Agriculture in Southeast Asia: A Human Ecology Perspective*, edited by Gerald G. Marten. Boulder: Westview Press.

A Pronouncing Gazetteer and Geographical Dictionary of the Philippine Islands, United States of America. 1902. Prepared in the Bureau of Insular Affairs, War Department. Washington: Government Printing Office.

Pungayan, Eufronio L. 1980. Kinship Structures among Benguet Ibalois. *St Louis Research Journal* 11:1-59.

Radcliffe-Brown, A.R. 1950. "Introduction." In *African Systems of Kinship and Marriage*, edited by A.R. Radcliffe-Brown and Daryll Forde, 1-85. London: Oxford University Press.

Rambo, A. Terry. 1973. *A Comparison of Peasant Social Systems of Northern and Southern Vietnam: A Study of Ecological Adaptation, Social Succession and Cultural Evolution.* Carbondale: Southern Illinois University at Carbondale Press. Center for Vietnamese Studies, Monograph Series III.

Raymond, W.F. 1985. Options for Reducing Inputs to Agriculture: A Non-economist's View. *Journal of Agricultural Economics* 36:345-54.

Report of the Philippine Commission to the President. 1900-1901. 3 vols. Washington: Government Printing Office.

Reyes, Romana de los. 1980. *Managing Communal Gravity Systems: Farmers' Approaches and Implications for Program Planning.* Quezon City: Ateneo de Manila.

_____, M.F.P. Viado, S.B. Borlagdan and G. V. Gatdula. 1980. *Communal Gravity Systems: Four Case Studies.* Quezon City: Institute of Philippine Culture, Ateneo de Manila.

Richards, Carmen. 1950. *Death Stalks the Philippine Wilds: The Letters of Maud Huntley Jenks.* Minneapolis: The Lund Press.

Roberts, Simon. 1985. The Tswana Polity and "Tswana Law and Custom" Reconsidered. *Journal of Southern African Studies* 12:75-87.

Rodman, Margaret. 1984. Masters of Tradition: Customary Land Tenure and New Forms of Social Inequality in a Vanuatu Peasantry. *American Ethnologist* 11:61-80.

Rodman, William. 1982. "Gaps, Bridges and Levels of Law: Middlemen as Mediators in Vanuatu Society." In *Middlemen and Brokers in Oceania*, edited by W.L. Rodman and D.A. Counts, 69-95. Ann Arbor: University of Michigan Press.

_____. 1985. "A Law Unto Themselves": Legal Innovation in Ambae, Vanuatu. *American Ethnologist* 12:603-24.

Rosaldo, Renato. 1980. *Ilongot Headhunting: 1883-1974. A Study in Society and History.* Stanford: Stanford University Press.

Russell, Susan Diana. 1983. Entrepreneurs, Ethnic Rhetoric, and Economic Integration in Benguet Province, Highland Luzon, Philippines. Ph.D. dissertation. University of Illinois at Urbana-Champaign.

_____. 1987. Middlemen and Moneylending: Relations of Exchange in a Highland Philippine Economy. *Journal of Anthropological Research* 42:139-61.

Sadiay E Dinteg Ja Kuansia. 1984. *Random Activities: A Periodic Report from the Office of the Provincial Attorney*, vol. 1:14. Benguet Province.

Sahlins, Marshall. 1958. *Social Stratification in Polynesia.* Seattle: University of Washington Press.

Santos, B.D. 1982. "Law and Community: The Changing Nature of State Power in Late Capitalism." In *The Politics of Informal Justice.* Vol. 1, *The American Experience*, edited by R.L. Abel, 249-66. New York: Academic Press.

Scheerer, Otto. 1905. *The Nabaloi Dialect.* Department of the Interior Ethnological Survey Publication. Vol. 2, Part 2. Manila: Bureau of Public Printing.

Scheffler, H. W. 1964. Descent Concepts and Descent Groups: The Maori Case. *Journal of the Polynesian Society* 73:126-33.

Schneider, David M. 1984. *The Critique of the Study of Kinship.* Ann Arbor: University of Michigan Press.

Scott, James. 1985. *Weapons of the Weak*. New Haven: Yale University Press.

Scott, William Henry. 1974. *The Discovery of the Igorots*. Quezon City: New Day Publishers.

_____. 1975a. *German Travelers on the Cordillera (1860-1890)*. Manila: The Filipiana Book Guild.

_____. 1975b. *History on the Cordillera. Collected Writings on Mountain Province History*. Baguio City: Baguio Printing and Publishing Co.

Shipton, Parker. 1984. Lineage and Locality as Antithetical Principles in East African Systems of Land Tenure. *Ethnology* 23:117-32.

Silliman, G. Sidney. 1985. A Political Analysis of the Philippines' Katarungang Pambarangay System of Informal Justice through Mediation. *Law and Society Review* 19:279.

Smith, Clifford T. 1984. "Land Reform as a Pre-condition for Green Revolution in Latin America." In *Understanding Green Revolutions: Agrarian Change and Development Planning in South Asia*, edited by Tim Bayliss-Smith and Sudhir Wanmali, 18-36. Cambridge: Cambridge University Press.

Smith, M.G. 1975. *Corporations and Society: The Social Anthropology of Collective Action*. Chicago: Aldine.

Sonius, H.W.J. 1963. *Introduction to Aspects of Customary Land Law in Africa as Compared with Some Indonesian Aspects*. Leiden: Universitaire Pers Leiden.

Stoljar, S.J. 1975. *Groups and Estates: An Inquiry into Corporate Theory*. Canberra: Australian National University Press.

Stone, Alan. 1985. The Place of Law in the Marxian Structure-Superstructure Archetype. *Law and Society Review* 19:39-67.

Strathern, A.J. 1971. *The Rope of Moka*. Cambridge: Cambridge University Press.

Strouthes, Daniel. 1990. Association for Political and Legal Anthropology Column. *Anthropology Newsletter* 31(3):8-9.

Tapang, B.P., Jr. 1985. Innovation and Social Change: The Ibaloi Cattle Enterprise in Benguet. *Cordillera Studies Center Social Science Monograph Series* 5:1-54.

Tomosugi, Takahashi. 1980. *A Structural Analysis of Thai Economic History*. Tokyo: Institute of Developing Economics Occassional Paper Series No. 17.

Tonkinson, R. 1983. Working For the Judge: Role and Responsibility. *Anthropological Forum* 5:182-88.

Vanderlinden, Jacques. 1989. Return to Legal Pluralism: Twenty Years Later. *Journal of Legal Pluralism* 28:149-57.

Wade, Robert. 1987. The Management of Common Property Resources: Collective Action as an Alternative to Privatization or State Regulation. *Cambridge Journal of Economics* 11(2):95-106.

Wells, Miriam. 1987. Legal Conflict and Class Structure: The Independent Contractor-Employee Controversy in California Agriculture. *Law and Society Review* 21:49.

Westermark, George D. 1986. Court Is an Arrow: Legal Pluralism in Papua New Guinea. *Ethnology* 25:131-49.

Wiber, M.G. 1984. Corporate Groups in the Productive Technology of the Ibaloi: A Preliminary Report. *Cordillera Studies Center Monograph Series* 3: Folio 1:4-24.

_____. 1985. Dynamics of the Peasant Household Economy: Labor Recruitment and Allocation in an Upland Philippine Community. *Journal of Anthropological Research* 41(4):427-41.

_____. 1989. "The Cañao Imperative: Changes to Resource Control, Stratification and the Economy of Ritual among the Ibaloi, Northern Philippines." In *Changing Lives and Changing Rites: Ritual and Social Dynamics in Philippine and Indonesian Uplands*, edited by Susan Russell and Clark Cunningham, 45-62. Ann Arbor: University of Michigan Press.

_____. 1990a. Abandoning "Guilt Causes" in Social Theory: Conditions for and Consequences of Legal Pluralism in the Philippine Uplands. *Law and Anthropology* 5:43-65.

_____. 1990b Who Benefits from Custom? Jural Constraints on Land Accumulation and on Social Stratification in Benguet Province, Northern Philippines. *Journal of Southeast Asian Studies* 21(2):329-39.

_____. 1991. Levels of Property Rights, Levels of Law in Ibaloi (Philippine) Society: Challenging the Oversimplification of Non-Western Property Systems. *Man* 26(3):469-92.

_____, and June Prill-Brett. 1988. Perfecting Plural Societies: Lessons from the Comparative Study of Property Systems and Jural Disparity in Two Philippine Ethnic Minorities. *Culture* 8(1):21-34.

_____. 1991. Constraints on the Sharing of Power: Whose Self-Determination Shall Prevail? Issues from the Northern Philippines. Vol. 1. Compiled by Harald W. Finkler, 39-51. *Proceedings of the Commission on Folk Law and Legal Pluralism VIth International Symposium*, Ottawa August 14-18.

Wolf, E.R. 1957. Closed Corporate Peasant Communities in Meso America and Central Java. *Southwestern Journal of Anthropology* 13:1-18.

_____. 1982. *Europe and the People Without History*. Berkeley: University of California Press.

Woodman, G.R. 1983. How State Courts Create Customary Law in Ghana and Nigeria. Vol. 1. Compiled by Harald W. Finkler, 297-332. *Proceedings of the Folk Law and Legal Pluralism Symposium, XIth International Conference of Anthropological and Ethnological Sciences*, Vancouver, August 19-23.

Worchester, Dean C. 1906. The Non-Christian Tribes of Northern Luzon. *The Philippine Journal of Science* 1:791-875.

Index

159